MAR 2 5 2006

A Dream Deferred:

The Jim Crow Era

Lucent Library of Black History

Anne Wallace Sharp

LUCENT BOOKS

An imprint of Thomson Gale, a part of The Thomson Corporation

THOMSON
★
GALE

Detroit • New York • San Francisco • San Diego • New Haven, Conn.
Waterville, Maine • London • Munich

THOMSON
™
GALE

© 2005 Thomson Gale, a part of The Thomson Corporation.

Thomson and Star Logo are trademarks and Gale and Lucent Books are registered trademarks used herein under license.

For more information, contact
Lucent Books
27500 Drake Rd.
Farmington Hills, MI 48331-3535
Or you can visit our Internet site at http://www.gale.com

LIBRARY OF CONGRESS CATALOGING-IN-PUBLICATION DATA

Sharp, Anne Wallace.
    A dream deferred : the Jim Crow era / by Anne Wallace Sharp.
        p. cm. — (Lucent library of Black history)
    Includes bibliographical references and index.
    ISBN 1-59018-700-8 (hard cover : alk. paper)
    1. African Americans—Civil rights—Southern States—History—Juvenile literature.
2. African Americans—Segregation—Southern States—History—Juvenile literature.
3. African Americans—Legal status, laws, etc.—Southern States—History—Juvenile
literature. 4. Southern States—Race relations—Juvenile literature. 5. Racism—
Southern States—History—Juvenile literature. 6. African Americans—History—
1863–1877—Juvenile literature. 7. African Americans—History—1877–1964—Juvenile
literature. I. Title. II. Series.
E185.2.S53 2005
323.1196'073075'09034—dc22
                                                                            2005002799

Printed in the United States of America

#71
Westwood Branch
1246 Glendon Ave.
Los Angeles, CA 90024

Contents

Foreword

It has been more than five hundred years since Africans were first brought to the New World in shackles, and over 140 years since slavery was formally abolished in the United States. Over fifty years have passed since the fallacy of "separate but equal" was obliterated in the American courts, and some forty years since the watershed Civil Rights Act of 1965 guaranteed the rights and liberties of all Americans, especially those of color. Over time, these changes have become celebrated landmarks in American history. In the twenty-first century, African American men and women are politicians, judges, diplomats, professors, deans, doctors, artists, athletes, business owners, and home owners. For many, the scars of the past have melted away in the opportunities that have been found in contemporary society. Observers such as Peter N. Kirsanow, who sits on the U.S. Commission of Civil Rights, point to these accomplishments and conclude, "The growing black middle class may be viewed as proof that most of the civil rights battles have been won."

In spite of these legal victories, however, prejudice and inequality have persisted in American society. In 2003, African Americans comprised just 12 percent of the nation's population, yet accounted for 44 percent of its prison inmates and 24 percent of its poor. Racially motivated hate crimes continue to appear on the pages of major newspapers in many American cities. Furthermore, many African Americans still experience either overt or muted racism in their daily lives. A 1996 study undertaken by Professor Nancy Krieger of the Harvard School of Public Health, for example, found that 80 percent of the African American participants reported having experienced racial discrimination in one or more settings, including at work or school, applying for housing and medical care, from the police or in the courts, and on the street or in a public setting.

It is for these reasons that many believe the struggle for racial equality and justice is far from over. These episodes of discrimination threaten to shatter the illusion that America has completely overcome its racist past, causing many black Americans to become increasingly frustrated and confused. Scholar and writer Ellis Cose has described this splintered state in the following way: "I have done everything I was supposed to do. I have stayed out of trouble with the law, gone to the right schools, and worked myself nearly to death. What more do they want? Why in God's name won't they accept me as a full human being?" For Cose and others, the struggle for equality and justice has yet to be fully achieved.

In many subtle yet important ways, the traumatic experiences of slavery and segregation continue to inform the way race is discussed and experienced in the twenty-first century. Indeed, it is possible that America will always grapple with the fallout from its distressing past. Ulric Haynes, dean of the Hofstra University School of Business has said, "Perhaps race will always matter, given the historical circumstances under which we came to this country." But studying this past and understanding how it contributes to present-day dialogues about race and history in America is a critical component of contemporary education. To this end, the Lucent Library of Black History offers a thorough look at the experiences that have shaped the black community and the American people as a whole. Annotated bibliographies provide readers with ideas for further research, while fully documented primary and secondary source quotations enhance the text. Each book in the series explores a different episode of black history; together they provide students with a wealth of information as well as launching points for further study and discussion.

A Dream Deferred

For the approximately 4 million African American slaves living in the South at the end of the Civil War, the North's victory in 1865 brought freedom. With this freedom came the hope of the full rights and privileges of citizenship that other Americans had long enjoyed. For the newly freed slaves, those rights were guaranteed by the Fourteenth and Fifteenth Amendments to the Constitution and by a number of laws enacted by Congress. Freedom and equality mandated by the law, however, did not extend into the daily lives of African Americans. Resistance among Southern whites caused the hopes and dreams of African Americans for equality in any practical sense to be deferred for nearly a hundred years.

Slavery and the Civil War

Slavery in America had been practiced since colonial times, long before the United States existed as an independent nation. Seeking an inexpensive labor force, European colonists brought thousands of people from Africa to the New World to work on tobacco and sugar plantations. The Africans did not come willingly; they were taken by force from their native villages, sold to the highest bidder, and shipped to the New World in chains. Those who did not perish during the crossing of the Atlantic Ocean were then sold again to plantation owners, who put them to work in their fields and homes.

Those held in slavery were completely at the mercy of their white masters. Slaves had no control over the hours they worked, endured beatings and other forms of punishment, and could be separated from family members at the whim of the owner. Slavery was, moreover, a lifelong condition; only in the rarest instances did a slaveowner grant freedom to his or her slaves. It took four years of bloody civil warfare to bring an end to slavery in the United States.

White Domination

The South's slaveowners were forced by the victorious North to accept the end of slavery, yet still they sought to continue their domination of blacks. Not content with just wanting to control the former slaves, white Southerners sought to prevent African Americans

Plantation owners in Florida bid on a slave on the auction block. Throughout the South, plantation owners purchased slaves to work in their vast fields and homes.

from exercising any of the rights that had been granted them following the Civil War. The result, in the late nineteenth century, was a system of laws and practices called Jim Crow. Throughout the South, laws were enacted that severely limited African Americans' rights and privileges.

The enactment of myriad Jim Crow laws in the late nineteenth century ended for more than half a century the hope that African Americans could achieve equality with whites. The laws discrim-

African American children attend class at a segregated school in Virginia in the 1940s. Segregation was a fact of life for Southern blacks throughout the Jim Crow era.

inated against blacks in every phase of life, from forbidding them a seat with whites in streetcars to denying them access to most types of medical care. Historian Roy L. Brooks elaborates: "African Americans under both slavery and Jim Crow lived in a state of abject, absolute inequality. In all spheres of life, they had less than whites: less income, wealth, occupational prestige, housing, education, and political influence."[1]

The Concept of Racism

Underlying the Jim Crow system was racism, or the belief that whites are superior in all ways to other races. Throughout the United States, but particularly in the South, this idea was ingrained in the hearts and minds of whites. As a consequence, for nearly one hundred years after the end of the Civil War, African Americans were unable to participate fully in the American Dream. As late as the early 1940s, thanks to the effects of the Jim Crow system, 90 percent of all African American families lived in poverty, and fewer than 5 percent of black Southerners could vote.

Segregation, moreover, was practiced routinely throughout the United States. Even in the North, where there were no Jim Crow laws, discrimination remained a fact of life. Many jobs and even entire industries were within the province of only one race or another. Historian David M. Kennedy observes, "Most African Americans on the eve of World War II lived lives scarcely different from those to which their freedmen forbears had been consigned after the Civil War."[2]

African American dreams of equality and freedom were repeatedly denied during the Jim Crow era as white supremacy reigned. Those dreams, however, did not die. Roger Wilkins, an African American scholar and assistant attorney general under President Lyndon B. Johnson, writing in the early twenty-first century, commented on these dreams and the discrimination he and other blacks had faced growing up in the South: "For blacks, it was a question of identity and deep emotionalism as well. We were clear that we were fully human and were profoundly offended by the continuing attempts to disable and diminish us by withholding aspects of our American birth right."[3] Until the latter half of the twentieth century, however, the dreams of millions of black Americans would be deferred.

Chapter One

Maintaining White Supremacy

After the end of the Civil War on April 9, 1865, over 4 million African Americans found themselves free. The slaves had actually been formally freed more than two years earlier in the Emancipation Proclamation issued by President Abraham Lincoln. The Proclamation, however, resulted in very few slaves actually being set free. Lincoln's decree applied only to those slaves living in the Confederacy, in states where it could not yet be enforced. Slaves living in states that had remained loyal to the Union were not covered at all. Only with the war's end could African Americans hope that their long-held dreams of freedom and equality would finally come true.

The end of slavery sent shudders of fear through the hearts of white Southerners. In the wake of their defeat in the Civil War, Southerners were confronted not only with the hated Northern occupying forces but with the presence of thousands of newly freed slaves, whose feelings toward their former masters could hardly be expected to be benign. No longer able to force blacks to work without pay or dictate their every move, white Southerners looked for new ways to maintain control over blacks.

Presidential Reconstruction

Southern whites had reason to hope that the federal government would be sympathetic to their concerns. Even Lincoln, who had made the abolition of slavery the moral centerpiece of the North's war effort, was prepared to offer amnesty to most Southerners. He had also shown himself inclined to move slowly toward giving blacks the vote. Lincoln, moreover, had demonstrated his determination to persuade the radical elements within the Republican-controlled Congress not to punish the former Confederacy harshly. Furthermore, the assassination of Lincoln on April 14, 1865, left the presidency in the hands of a Southerner, Andrew Johnson, who openly opposed expanding or protecting the rights of the newly freed slaves.

During the period known to historians as Presidential Reconstruction (1865–1867), Johnson's hands-off policies resulted in conditions for African Americans in the South changing little from those during slavery's heyday. Conditions remained so bad for blacks in the South that journalist Carl Shurz reported in 1866, "Wherever I go, the street, the shop, the house, or the steamboat,

In this illustration, Abraham Lincoln reads the Emancipation Proclamation to his cabinet. The proclamation freed Southern slaves two years before the end of the Civil War.

I hear the people talk in such a way as to indicate that they are yet to conceive of the Negro as possessing any rights at all."[4]

The Black Codes

Left largely to themselves, many Southern states' policies regarding blacks were virtually identical to those in the prewar South. Between 1865 and 1867 Southern governments, one after another, instituted rules, called the Black Codes, to govern the conduct of the freedmen. These laws were much like rules, or slave codes, followed during slavery's heyday. In many cases, in the new laws the word "slave" was simply replaced by the word "black." The Black Codes were enforced by a police apparatus and judicial system in which African Americans had virtually no voice or power.

While the laws differed slightly from state to state, in general the Black Codes prohibited African Americans from owning land, imposed nighttime curfews, and established punishments for gestures, acts, and behaviors that whites could find insulting. Mississippi and South Carolina established the first and most severe of the Black Codes toward the end of 1865. Mississippi, for example, required all African Americans to possess, each January, written evidence of employment for the upcoming year. Those who left their jobs or were unemployed were subject to arrest. South Carolina forbade African Americans from holding any job other than farming or domestic service unless they paid a yearly tax that ranged from ten to one hundred dollars, a fee that few blacks could afford.

Among the harshest laws were the vagrancy codes that governed the employment of African Americans. Historian Philip Dray describes these laws: "The most pernicious of the codes were the vagrancy laws under which any person not lawfully employed could be arrested, hired out to the highest bidder, and kept in virtual bondage until he had paid off his fine."[5] According to these laws vagrants included those who were unemployed, disorderly, and even those who misspent what they had earned. The vagrancy laws led to the arrests of hundreds of thousands of African Americans, most of whom were then sentenced to work on the same plantations where they had been enslaved.

The vagrancy codes even applied to children. "An especially outrageous part of the codes permitted black children to be kept as unpaid apprentice labor," writes historian Robert E. Martin. "If

The Fourteenth Amendment

■

During Reconstruction three amendments were added to the U.S. Constitution. These amendments were all aimed at providing freedom and equality to the nation's millions of African Americans. The Thirteenth Amendment, passed December 6, 1865, ended slavery, while the Fifteenth Amendment, passed on February 3, 1870, gave blacks the right to vote. Despite the importance of these two amendments, however, it was the Fourteenth Amendment that caused the most controversy and concern in the South.

Passed on July 9, 1868, the Fourteenth Amendment granted African Americans their full citizenship. The amendment was designed to protect the civil liberties of the recently freed slaves. In addition, the amendment specifically forbade any state to deny any of the rights inherent in citizenship to any individual. It also stated that all citizens were to have the equal protection of the law in applying these rights. Since its passage during Reconstruction, the Fourteenth Amendment, and specifically the equal protection clause, has been applied in a number of ground-breaking court cases.

black parents were decided to be unfit parents by white authorities, their children were bound over to white farmers, frequently their former owners, until the children reached the age of twenty-one."[6] Again, the effect was to reenslave young blacks. White landowners could refuse to hire young blacks. The youth were then declared wards of the state and forced to earn their keep by working for the same people who had refused to hire them as paid labor.

Radical Reconstruction

Outraged that Johnson's leniency toward the South allowed such practices to continue, the so-called Radical Republicans in Congress fought for a harsher approach to Reconstruction. Led by Senator Charles Sumner and Representative Thaddeus Stevens, the Radicals pushed a series of laws through Congress in 1866 and 1867 called the Reconstruction Acts. These laws required Southern states to dissolve their governments and write new constitutions in which African Americans were given equal rights. The United States then entered a period of history known as Radical Reconstruction (1867 to 1877), during which white Southerners were much more subject to federal control.

The new constitutions that were written in accordance with the Reconstruction Acts outlawed the Black Codes, gave the vote to African Americans, and included provisions that guaranteed the civil rights of all citizens, black and white. Federal troops were stationed throughout the South to ensure that these new rights were respected. These rights were further guaranteed by the passage of the Fourteenth Amendment in 1868, which, while not specifically mentioning blacks, granted citizenship to all Americans and guaranteed equal protection under the law.

African Americans in Political Office

The new state constitutions also guaranteed that African Americans were eligible to hold political office. As a consequence, a few African Americans were elected to a number of important positions. For instance, in 1870 South Carolina became the first Southern state to send an African American, Joseph H. Rainey, to the United States Congress. In fact, South Carolina held the distinction of being the state where African Americans exercised the greatest influence. In the first post–Civil War state legislature, there were eighty-seven blacks and forty whites. Yet despite this African American majority, the governor and most of the other leadership roles in the state government remained firmly in white hands.

Between 1869 and 1910 two African Americans became U.S. senators and twenty held seats in the U.S. House of Representatives. The two senators were Hiram R. Revels and Blanche K. Bruce, both from Mississippi. Bruce was particularly noteworthy in that he introduced a number of bills to the Senate in an effort to improve conditions for African Americans in the South. Several of the African American congressmen served multiple terms.

Other African Americans held important positions within various state and local governments. These positions included an associate justice of a state supreme court, a secretary of state, a district attorney, various sheriffs, and mayors. Despite the prestige that went with these positions, the men who held these offices had little real power to effect lasting change in the South. For example, whenever they attempted to introduce important legislation that would benefit the black community, white leaders worked behind the scenes to defeat the measures. In addition, if African American sheriffs arrested white offenders, all-white juries and a legal system dominated by whites meant that whites were rarely convicted of crimes committed against blacks.

Broken Promises

In reality, despite the new state constitutions and the election of blacks to political office, the everyday lives of African Americans changed little. In part this was due to a failure of the federal government to follow through on commitments it had made to the freed slaves. For instance, after the Civil War the federal government had promised all African Americans forty acres of land but only gave a few acres to a relative handful of blacks. African American farmers, facing poverty and starvation, were forced to work

Hiram R. Revels (left) and Blanche K. Bruce (right) were the first black senators, both elected in the state of Mississippi in the 1870s.

The Freedmen's Bureau

Despite the heavily entrenched racial attitudes in the South, the federal government was able to find ways to improve the lives of the former slaves. The Bureau of Refugees, Freedmen, and Abandoned Lands (known generally as the Freedmen's Bureau) was founded on March 3, 1865, under the direction of the War Department. One of this agency's primary functions was to provide for the welfare of African Americans. Over the course of seven years, the Freedmen's Bureau created more than forty hospitals, distributed over 20 million meals to the hungry, and encouraged black voting and political involvement.

The agency made its biggest impact on African American life, however, in the field of education through the creation of over four thousand black schools. At the request of the bureau, several Protestant groups from the North sent teachers to the South along with donations of books and money for use by the bureau. One such group was the American Baptist Home Mission Society, an organization that founded three African American colleges in the South: Morehouse College and Spelman College in Georgia and Shaw University in North Carolina. For the first time in their history African Americans in the South had access to education. By the end of Reconstruction over two hundred and fifty thousand blacks were attending school.

Two teachers with the Freedmen's Bureau teach recently freed slaves to read in a Virginia school.

for their former masters, earning barely enough money to keep their families alive. Historians John Hope Franklin and Alfred A. Moss Jr. explain: "Because the federal government failed to give blacks much land, they slowly returned to the farms and resumed work under circumstances scarcely more favorable than those prevailing before the war."[7]

Wherever and whenever African Americans tried to open businesses, attend school, vote, or travel, they were often subject to humiliation, intimidation, and violence. Despite the presence of federal troops in the South and the government's promise to uphold blacks rights, few African Americans were able to exercise those rights. Black businesses and schools were burned, black children attempting to attend school were harassed and often physically intimidated, and those African Americans who attempted to enter white establishments were denied admission. Hundreds of thousands of blacks were victims of violence at the hands of white Southerners. Violence against African Americans, in fact, reached staggering proportions as white Southerners sought to exercise absolute control over blacks by any means possible.

Return to Southern Control

The ability of African Americans to exercise their civil rights was further impaired by a waning interest on the part of the federal government in protecting black citizens. Contending with high inflation and a growing national debt, the federal government was less and less able to afford the expense of Reconstruction. As a result of urgent financial needs elsewhere, the government began to phase out its intervention in the South. This loss of interest turned into a "do-nothing" policy toward African Americans and their problems in the South.

The federal government's declining interest in the South coincided with a return of Southern Democrats to positions of power that transplanted Republican Northerners had held. Southerners accomplished this in large part by manipulating and intimidating black voters, who tended to vote Republican. North Carolina, Tennessee, and Virginia were all under Democratic control by 1870, with Texas, Alabama, and Arkansas following shortly thereafter. Democrats were also able to gain control of Mississippi in 1875 following an election marred by violence. During the election whites patrolled the polling places and voting booths, threatening black would-be voters and tearing up ballots submitted by those African Americans who did vote. As a result, the Democrats won easily. Yazoo County, Mississippi, was just one of many locales where Republicans experienced such a reversal of fortune. A few years earlier African American votes for Republican candidates totaled twenty-five hundred; in 1875 only seven votes for Republicans were counted. The story was similar elsewhere.

Finally, however, it was a Republican president who put an end to Reconstruction and federal efforts to protect Southern blacks' civil rights. The presidential election of 1876 was a bitterly contested one between Republican Rutherford B. Hayes and Democrat Samuel Tilden. Tilden won the popular vote by a slim margin but thanks to disputes over the results in a number of Southern states, neither candidate managed to win a majority of the electoral votes. As required by the Constitution, Congress, where Southerners held many seats, decided the election. In secret negotiations, Hayes promised Southern members of Congress that he would end Reconstruction in return for being declared the winner of the disputed election. Hayes became president on March 4, 1877, and soon kept his word, ordering the withdrawal of federal troops from the South.

Disenfranchisement

Following the end of Reconstruction, Southern politicians moved quickly to eliminate many of the rights that African Americans had been granted. White Southerners reasoned that as long as African Americans remained able to vote, they would be in a position to affect the political process and maintain a say in the governing of the South. The first goal of many Southern politicians, therefore, was to stop blacks from voting. Historian David R. Goldfield explains: "The restriction, dilution, or outright elimination of black suffrage was essential for restoring the old order."[8]

During the next few years Southern states passed laws that kept most African Americans from voting. For instance, would-be voters were required to own at least three hundred dollars worth of property, a requirement that few African Americans could meet. Since thousands of white Southerners also fell short of this criterion, however, a loophole (known as a "grandfather clause") was

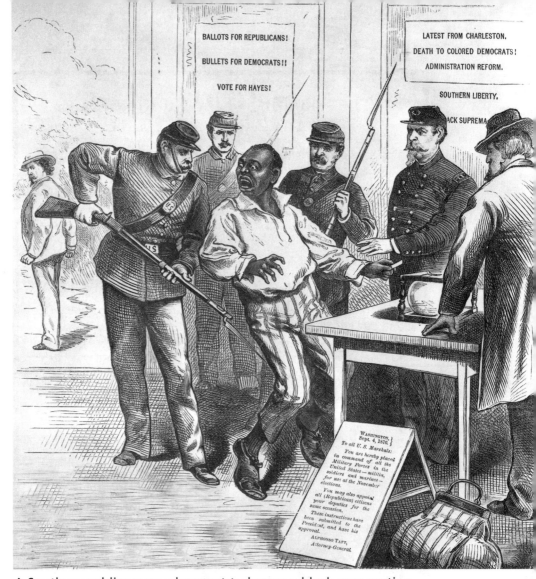

A Southern soldier uses a bayonet to harass a black man casting his vote. Throughout the late nineteenth century, Southern whites used violence to keep blacks from the polls.

provided. These clauses, written into many state constitutions, exempted from the property requirements men whose grandfathers had voted. Since most African Americans' grandfathers had been slaves, they had never voted, so most black would-be voters were automatically disqualified.

Literacy requirements disqualified thousands of other African Americans, since most had little or nothing in the way of education. The literacy tests included nonsensical questions like "How high is up?" and "How many bubbles in a bar of soap?" designed to disqualify

The Founding of the Ku Klux Klan

The need among whites to maintain supremacy in the South and the desire of Southerners to prevent blacks from attaining equality led to the rapid growth of secret organizations such as the Ku Klux Klan, the Knights of the White Camellia, and the White Brotherhood. The largest of these groups was the Klan. First organized in 1866 in Pulaski, Tennessee, as a social group for former Confederate veterans, the Klan, within a few months, became a terrorist group intent on maintaining white supremacy by any and all means. Similar organizations soon spread to every state in the South and included mayors, judges, planters, and law enforcement officers in their membership.

The Klan effectively terrorized scores of African Americans merely by their presence. Espousing the need for white domination and active during the years of Reconstruction, the Klan used violence to disrupt elections and the efforts of the federal government to enforce the civil rights of African Americans throughout the South. The Klan burned down blacks' homes, churches, and businesses and beat, bullied, intimidated, and killed thousands of blacks throughout the South. In the worst-affected counties, disguised Klan members ranged throughout the countryside on a regular basis, dragging blacks from their homes, burning their houses, and then either driving them away or killing them.

Disguised Klan members pose with their weapons in this nineteenth-century illustration.

even those who could read and write. Other African Americans were asked to translate passages from Chinese newspapers into English or quote long passages from the state constitution.

These property and literacy requirements effectively left African Americans virtually powerless to affect decision making in the South. James K. Vardaman, a Mississippi politician, explained in 1890 that this had been the point of instituting such requirements all along: "The Mississippi constitution convention . . . was held for no other purpose than to eliminate the nigger from politics."[9]

The few who managed to overcome the barriers posed by property and literacy requirements faced still another impediment—the threat of violence that had always been used against blacks who in any way displeased whites. A Southerner from Georgia explained: "We don't stop [a] colored from voting if he want to vote, but a bullet would follow him out the door."[10] Thousands of African American voters stopped going to the polls because they feared they would be killed if they did so.

Playing a key role in keeping African Americans from the polls were white supremacist groups such as the Ku Klux Klan and the Knights of the White Camellia. These groups, whose primary goal was to maintain white supremacy by any means at their disposal, had been organized during the early days of Reconstruction. Using threats of violence—and murder if the threats failed—the Klan and other groups terrorized black communities and kept hundreds of thousands of blacks away from the polling places.

Supreme Court Cases

Southern whites got some crucial help from the U.S. Supreme Court, which began striking down many of the laws that had been passed to protect African Americans. The decisions of the Court all served to limit the federal government's power to enforce the newly passed Fourteenth and Fifteenth Amendments. In the so-called Slaughterhouse Cases of 1873, for instance, the Court decreed that individuals could not turn to the federal government for help when their civil rights were abused. Then in *United States v. Cruikshank*, a case heard in 1876, the Court further ruled that the federal government could not intervene in state or local court cases. Effectively, this isolated African Americans from the legal protection of the federal government.

More destructive yet, in *Reese v. United States* in 1876, the Court ruled that the Fifteenth Amendment, which had given African Americans the right to vote, did not give the federal government the power to enforce the actual ability of blacks to vote. This ruling, in effect, enabled Southern state and local governments to disenfranchise African Americans with the tacit approval of the federal government. A few years later, the Supreme Court also upheld literacy and property requirements for voting. These rulings were followed in 1883 by the Supreme Court declaring the Civil Rights Act of 1875 unconstitutional. This landmark legislation had prohibited discrimination in public places and had promised equal rights to all Americans.

The end of Reconstruction and the return of white Southerners to power shattered the dreams of African Americans. Southern whites were able to reverse or nullify most of the laws that had provided equal rights to the former slaves. By the end of the nineteenth century, in fact, African Americans found themselves in a situation not much different from slavery.

Reconstruction had been a period of great hope—and crushing disappointment. The end of bondage that African Americans had been seeking for so long did not bring with it equality and true freedom. White supremacy had been maintained and strengthened and would dominate every aspect of Southern life for the next ninety years.

Chapter Two

Separate but Equal: The Jim Crow System

During the last two decades of the nineteenth century, white Southerners had strengthened their own position while taking away the rights of African Americans to vote and hold office. This was not enough in the minds of many Southerners to adequately preserve white supremacy. Not content with relying on the unwritten racial code that existed in the South, white politicians moved forward with a plan to enshrine in law the racism and discrimination that already existed.

Southern Support of Segregation

White Southerners had long limited the opportunities of African Americans and discriminated against them in every aspect of life. Blacks were relegated to the most subservient jobs and forced to acknowledge the superiority of whites in all social interactions. Unwritten but nonetheless official racial codes in the South forbade the teaching of reading and writing to black children; nor were African Americans allowed to interact on an equal basis with whites. The best education, the best homes, jobs, and public services were for whites only.

As a result of this discrimination, by the time most whites attained adulthood they were imbued with the belief that African Americans were inferior to whites in every way. Goldfield notes: "They came to accept the inferior, demeaning status of blacks as a natural element of the Southern landscape."[11] At the same time, white Southerners convinced themselves that this separation from African Americans was the key to their own society's survival.

Believing that no less than the preservation of white society was at stake, Southerners took steps to write segregation into law. Moreover, because the federal government and Northern politicians had adopted a hands-off attitude toward the South, white Southerners were free to move forward with their plans without interference.

Theories on Race

White Southerners were aided in their plans to lock in segregation by an emerging national consensus on race. By the end of the nineteenth century many humanitarians, scientists, and other educated people had convinced themselves that African Americans and other "people of color" were innately inferior. As such, nonwhites were thought incapable of social advancement, impossible to educate, and unworthy of a role in governing. Scientist Francis Galton brought these beliefs, collectively referred to as eugenics, before the general public in the 1870s. Eugenicists subscribed to the theory that intelligence and leadership skills were genetically determined traits. Eugenicists also believed that these traits were prevalent only in what they termed the "better and superior races"—in other words, whites.

Some prominent biologists took Galton's theory further, espousing the view that blacks were only one step removed from apes. Meanwhile, scholars justified the inferior social status of African Americans by proposing that blacks had been happiest under the slave system and that they were lost without the guidance of their white masters. Historian Adam Fairclough elaborates: "Many whites professed amazement that blacks were surviving at all, grimly predicting that, like the Indians, they had no long-term future as a race."[12]

The claim of black inferiority was spread by popular writers in blatantly racist terms. Author Hinton R. Helper, for instance, in

Racial Stereotypes and Myths

A central tenet of white supremacy was that blacks were inferior and therefore not deserving of respect by the rest of society. Among the characterizations used by Southern whites against African Americans were that blacks were mentally inferior, lazy, and slow moving. White Southerners also frequently described blacks as childlike and incapable of taking care of themselves. Historian David R. Goldfield in his book *Black, White and Southern* elaborates, stating that white Southerners believed "blacks are poor and shiftless and behave in certain ways because that is the way they are, and they are happy that way."

The American media, Southern writers, and even advertisers of the times reinforced this stereotype. Author Joel Chandler Harris in his Uncle Remus stories, for instance, helped perpetuate the myth of black inferiority, while newspapers and other writers frequently described African Americans in derogatory terms. With these stereotypes, white Southerners could rationalize that segregation was in the best interest of African Americans. And, using the argument that blacks could not really take care of themselves, Southerners easily justified the Jim Crow system as a humane way to take care of blacks.

In this nineteenth-century stereotypical Currier & Ives print, a young black couple tries to elope on a bucking bull as the father rushes from the house with a shotgun.

1867 accused African Americans of having many natural defects and deformities: "He [a black man] is cursed with a black complexion, an apish aspect, and a wooly head; he is also rendered odious by an intolerable stench, a thick skull, and a booby brain."[13] Writer Charles Carroll in his book *The Negro Is a Beast* took these views one step further by declaring that African Americans were not really human beings at all.

Southern leaders were quick to add their own voices in support of such claims. In 1913 Thomas Bailey, a Southern educator, made these remarks: "The white race must dominate. The Negro is inferior and will remain so. . . . Let the lowest white man count for more than the highest Negro."[14] Bailey supported his remarks by claiming that these facts were God-ordained and used the Bible to defend his theories. John Temple Graves, an Atlanta editor, agreed: "This is our [white man's] country. . . . The Negro is an accident—an unwilling, a blameless, but an unwholesome, unwelcome, helpless, unassimilable element in our civilization."[15]

A campaign poster from the 1860s depicts an idle black man profiting from the labor of hard-working white men, whose taxes go to support the Freedmen's Bureau.

Jim Crow

White politicians in the South were quick to take advantage of the prevailing opinions about race. Beginning in 1875, even before the formal end of Reconstruction, Southern legislatures one after another began writing new constitutions and new laws sanctioning the separation of the two races and strengthening white supremacy. These measures, known as the Jim Crow laws, by 1914 had been passed in every Southern state.

The Jim Crow laws applied to every facet of life in the South. Many public places were simply off-limits to blacks, while others were strictly segregated according to race. There were, for instance, segregated waiting rooms, lunch counters, prisons, public parks, restaurants, cemeteries, and hospitals. Theaters had separate entrances—a well-lighted and inviting front door for whites and a doorway opening onto the alley for African Americans. Once inside, white patrons sat downstairs while blacks were relegated to the back rows of the balcony. Everywhere restrooms were segregated, as were drinking fountains. Many facilities, such as amusement parks, roller-skating rinks, bowling alleys, swimming pools, and tennis courts, were designated for whites only. A few cities and states required separate boating and fishing areas for the two races.

Segregation was also widely practiced in the workplace. Most white-owned businesses refused to hire any African American workers at all. In the few that did, African Americans were not allowed to use the same doorways, stairs, or elevators that whites used. Neither could blacks use the same equipment as their white coworkers. Many factory owners required their black employees to work in separate areas of the building and forbade any interaction with white workers.

The Jim Crow system also applied to social interactions between the two races. Churches were strictly segregated with separate areas for white and black worshippers. African Americans were prohibited from shaking hands with white people, dancing with them, and playing checkers or dominoes with whites. Arkansas had separate gambling tables, while Oklahoma had segregated telephone booths.

Visual evidence of the Jim Crow laws was evident throughout the South. Signs were hung in store windows reminding African

Americans that it was against the law to try on clothes in stores patronized by whites. In addition, many laundries throughout the South refused to accept African Americans' laundry, hanging signs that read "We Wash for White People Only."

Virtually no facet of life (or death) was overlooked. Separate Bibles were even used for the swearing in of the two races in courthouses throughout the South. Blacks were forbidden to use the same sidewalks that whites used; once automobiles came into use, black drivers could not pass a buggy or wagon if the driver was white. There were even separate gallows in many states. Roger Wilkins summed up the situation he faced growing up in the later years of the Jim Crow era: "I was born in a segregated hospital in Kansas City in 1932 and my father was buried in a segregated cemetery there in 1941. Virtually everything in between was also segregated." [16]

Transportation

Many of the earliest Jim Crow laws applied to the field of transportation. Doors at train depots, ticket windows, waiting rooms, and toilet facilities, for instance, were all segregated. Always the facilities for blacks were inferior to those reserved for whites. For instance, waiting rooms for African Americans had no heat in winter, no fans in summer, and the furniture, consisting of broken chairs, was unusable.

Once on a train, African Americans found the accommodations even worse. There was no stool for black passengers to use when boarding or leaving trains, so no matter how old or infirm, they had to jump or climb on or off; the only help they could hope for would be from a fellow passenger. The cars blacks were relegated to were usually the oldest ones in service. In addition, the "colored" car was located at the end of the train where the soot from the coal-burning engine tended to land. It also served as the car where passengers went to smoke, making it the dirtiest and smelliest on the train. Often unruly white passengers, looking to alleviate their own boredom, would come and insult, humiliate, or beat African American passengers. When this happened, the victims of the white ruffians had no recourse: The conductor would never intervene.

No matter an African American's education or wealth, on a Southern train he or she was subject to such mistreatment. African American author and political activist W.E.B. DuBois was a victim of this

The Origins of the Term "Jim Crow"

The term "Jim Crow" had come into use as early as the 1830s. The term was taken from a minstrel show character created in 1830 by white entertainer Thomas "Daddy" Rice. He apparently saw a small black boy singing a popular song called *Jump Jim Crow.* The lyrics, according to the Internet article "The Origin of Jim Crow," included the following line: "Weel about and turn jis so, eb'ry time I weel about I jump Jim Crow." Rice copied the song and dance he had seen and then performed it in his own minstrel show.

To play the part of Jim Crow, an elderly black man, Rice wore blackface, or makeup that mocked the appearance of black skin,

and overexaggerated and mimicked the antics of the young boy. The Jim Crow character became so popular that white audiences soon linked the name to that of any black man. Gradually the name came to be applied to all the laws and customs that kept whites and African Americans separated.

Thomas "Daddy" Rice performs as Jim Crow in this illustration from *Harper's* magazine.

kind of discrimination when he rode a train in the South. He describes the conditions he and fellow passengers experienced:

> At an unattended window marked "colored" . . . an African American has to stand and stand and wait until every white

Despite his reputation as an eminent scholar, W.E.B DuBois was not exempt from the humiliating statutes of the Jim Crow era.

person at the other window is waited on. When the agent finally decides to serve the black passenger, he harasses and contradicts . . . gives many persons the wrong change, compels some to purchase their tickets on a train at a higher price, and sends you and me out onto the platform, burning with indignation and hatred. [17]

African Americans also found that in any dispute involving public transportation they would end up the loser. For instance, Ida B. Wells, an African American author, editor, and political activist, was forcibly removed from a streetcar in Memphis, Tennessee, in

1884 and arrested after refusing to give up her seat after she sat down in the white section of the car. She sued the streetcar company and was initially awarded damages of two hundred dollars. The decision was later reversed and Wells had to repay the money. Wells was outraged that the American legal system had betrayed her and wrote of this matter in her diary: "I have firmly believed all along that the law was on our side and would, when we appealed to it, give us justice. I feel shorn of that belief and utterly discouraged."[18]

Other forms of transportation proved just as difficult for African Americans. When automobiles became available in the early twentieth century, white policemen stopped hundreds of blacks driving down Southern streets. Frequently, black drivers, despite having broken no laws, saw their cars set on fire by white policemen and mobs. They themselves were often beaten and warned to give up driving. One white Georgia officer was heard telling an African American driver in 1917: "From now on, you niggers walk into town, or use that ole mule if you want to stay in this city."[19]

Traveling around the South from one town to another could also be trying for African Americans. Most hotels and inns were closed to blacks, so travelers had to stay with either friends or relatives. Their only other option was to sleep in their cars or by the side of the road, where they were often harassed or arrested for vagrancy. Traveling through unfamiliar territory also exposed blacks to Jim Crow laws that could differ from those they were familiar with. Blacks who came from Northern or Midwestern states where Jim Crow laws did not exist could readily find trouble when they unwittingly committed an offense. Ordering a meal in a white establishment, failing to move off a sidewalk to let a white person pass, or making some kind of gesture that whites perceived as insulting brought quick retaliation from white Southerners.

A black stranger in town could also be stopped and questioned any time by the police. If the black failed to convince a white police officer or even white civilians that he or she had legitimate business in town, the African American could be arrested and forcibly removed from town. Sometimes the stranger would simply be killed. After sunset many communities' streets were entirely off-limits to African Americans, who had to abide by strict curfews.

A black teacher lectures a disproportionately large group of students at a school in South Carolina. Black schools in the South were woefully inferior to white schools.

Education

Numerous Jim Crow laws were also enacted in the field of education. Shortly after the end of the Civil War, the federal agency created to help former slaves, the Freedmen's Bureau, had begun building schools for African Americans. However, efforts to provide much more than basic education to blacks in the South were adamantly opposed by white Southerners.

Southerners feared the aspirations that education might foster in African Americans. "They acquire uppishness, they begin to swell, and to fancy that they are equal to whites," stated one white Southern politician. "If you educate the Negroes, they won't stay where they belong."[20] Southern public officials, therefore, worked tirelessly to control and limit African Americans' education. Black schools, for instance, were forbidden to teach college preparation courses and were also required to teach the "white view" of history. This view glorified slavery and stressed the inferiority of the black race.

Public spending for African American schools was nearly nonexistent in many areas of the South. In North Carolina in the late 1920s, for instance, there was more money spent on school buses for white children than on African American education in total. Throughout the South, state governments spent nearly ten times the amount on educating whites than they did for blacks. Historians Franklin and Moss address this issue: "Nothing was more persistent in the first half of the twentieth century than the disparity between the money spent for the education of white children and that spent for the education of black children."[21]

As a result of the uneven spending, most African American schools bore little resemblance to white schools. Many students attended classes held in one-room shacks with cracked walls and leaky roofs. They sat on crude, backless benches, had few school supplies, little heating or light, no sanitary facilities, and few books. African American lawyer and civil rights activist Charles Hamilton Houston toured the South and talked of the primitive facilities he saw: "For toilet facilities, the boys have to cross the railroad and highway to get to the woods."[22] Schools for blacks were also usually understaffed. Teachers worked with children of all ages. Qualifications for teachers were minimal. Most African American teachers had less than an eighth grade education themselves.

Jim Crow in the North

Faced with discrimination at every turn, African Americans moved north in large numbers during the first three decades of the twentieth century in the hope that life would improve once they crossed the Mason-Dixon line. This hope was soon shattered as blacks realized that the North offered little if any prospect of improved conditions. While "White Only" and "Colored" signs might not be displayed as they were in the South, African Americans quickly became aware that segregation was still a fact of life in the North.

For example, African Americans were unable to find homes in most neighborhoods in the North. Instead, they were relegated to all-black neighborhoods with derogatory names like Boston's "Nigger Hill" or Cincinnati's "Little Africa." As was true in the South, some states and cities excluded African Americans from juries. In nearly every state, discrimination against blacks by hotels and restaurants was practiced and was perfectly legal. Schools, parks, and other taxpayer-supported facilities were segregated as well.

African Americans were also excluded from the majority of jobs in the North. Franklin and Moss elaborate: "Many white industrialists claimed that blacks were inefficient, while others refused to hire them because of objections raised by white employees."[23] This job discrimination forced the majority of African Americans to turn to the same kind of menial employment, serving as maids, janitors, and garbage collectors, that they had held in the South. Looking for equality in the North, African Americans found instead discrimination and hatred.

Plessy v. Ferguson

By the last decade of the nineteenth century, segregation had become so widely practiced that even the U.S. Supreme Court, when given the opportunity to strike down Jim Crow, instead held that segregation was permissible. The case before the Court, *Plessy v. Ferguson,* challenged a Louisiana law that prohibited African Americans from riding in the same railroad cars as whites. In 1892 Homer Adolph Plessy, a black passenger, had tried to sit in the section of a Louisiana train reserved for whites. Plessy had been forcibly removed from the train and arrested. After a Louisiana court ruled against him, Plessy appealed the decision all the way to the U.S. Supreme Court. The Court, however, ruled that Plessy had no right to ride in a car reserved for whites, thus endorsing the legality of segregation.

Justice Henry Billings Brown wrote the majority opinion of the Court:

> The object of the Fourteenth Amendment was undoubtedly to enforce the absolute equality of the two races before the law, but in the nature of things it could not have been intended to abolish distinctions based upon color, or to enforce social, as distinguished from political equality, or a commingling of the two races upon terms unsatisfactory to either.[24]

What this boiled down to was that as long as separate facilities —such as trains—were equal, segregation did not violate the Constitution of the United States.

The majority opinion further stated that it was not the federal government's job to correct social inequities: "If one race be inferior to the other socially, the Constitution of the United States cannot put them on the same plane."[25]

Segregation in the Military

The segregation that black youngsters experienced continued after they left school. For example, if a young man entered the military, he was the victim of some of the strictest segregation of all, despite the fact that Jim Crow laws were passed at the state, not national, level. African Americans serving in the military suffered the same discrimination that other blacks faced and were forced to contend with Jim Crow laws wherever they turned. Generally assigned the most menial of tasks, black soldiers were well aware of their status as second-class citizens.

During both World War I and World War II, African American soldiers in training were routinely insulted by their white officers, forced to live in separate and vastly inferior quarters, and given old and out-of-date weapons and other equipment. For example, at Montford Point, North Carolina, the home of the first black Marine Corps unit, African Americans had no uniforms, boots, or shoes, and were forced to spend their days cleaning toilets and hauling garbage. Historian Gail Buckley, in her book titled *American Patriots: The Story of Blacks in the Military,* describes the situation: "They were forced to stand naked at attention in the sun for hours . . . and ordered to memorize the Marine Corps manual, with more laws and rules than the Constitution."

A segregated black unit in South Korea waits to be deployed to the front during the Korean War.

A black man in Oklahoma drinks from a segregated water fountain.
The Supreme Court's ruling in the 1892 *Plessy v. Ferguson* case
upheld "separate but equal" laws in the United States.

Justice John Marshall Harlan was the lone dissenting voice on
the Court. He wrote that in respect to civil liberties all citizens were
equal before the law. He also accurately predicted that the majority's opinion in the *Plessy* case would not serve either race well:
"The destinies of the two races of this country are indissolubly
linked together, and the interests of both require that the common
government of all shall not permit the seeds of race hate to be plant-
ed under the sanction of law." [26] For most African Americans, especially those living in the South, the Supreme Court decision merely underscored what they already knew from personal experience:
that they could expect no help from their government in dealing
with racism and segregation.

Separate but Equal

In the wake of *Plessy v. Ferguson,* "separate but equal" became the
official doctrine of the South. Although separate facilities had long

been a fact of life, they were, however, rarely equal. In essence, the Jim Crow laws relegated blacks to second-class citizenship. African American civil rights activist William Pickens commented in 1923 on the Jim Crow system: "There is no such thing as a fair and just Jim Crow system with equal accommodation. . . . The inspiration of Jim Crow is a feeling of caste and a desire to 'keep in its place,' that is, to degrade the weaker group."[27]

In some ways the Supreme Court's ruling left African Americans even worse off than they had been when white supremacists used violence to enforce the old Black Codes. Whereas the Black Codes had dealt mostly with social matters, the Jim Crow laws

---

Benjamin "Pap" Singleton and the Kansas Experiment

Reacting to the end of Reconstruction and the introduction of the Jim Crow laws, many African Americans chose to leave the South. Benjamin "Pap" Singleton was one of the leaders of a group of blacks who moved to Kansas in the late nineteenth century in search of a better life. Born into slavery, Singleton lived in Tennessee and worked as a carpenter and a coffin maker. Making coffins for the thousands of black victims of white violence, Singleton came to the conclusion that there was little hope of equality in the South. He encouraged other African Americans to follow him to Kansas to see if they could find land there. Believing that he was carrying out God's plan for his people, he established Singleton Colony in Morris County, Kansas. His colony survived and prospered for several decades before declining in the early twentieth century.

Singleton's efforts led to the formation of other black colonies in Kansas, including the well-known African American community of Nicodemus, founded by a group of blacks from Lexington, Kentucky. Owing largely to the construction of the Missouri Pacific Railroad, blacks in Nicodemus found plenty of work and the town flourished in the late nineteenth century. The town was designated a National Landmark in 1975 and stands today as the only entirely African American community in Kansas.

deprived blacks of the means of civic participation and established segregated educational and transportation facilities. The economic system left African Americans in poverty and with little hope for improvement. In the long run even the law and court system had failed them.

The Jim Crow laws created a world framed by "whites only" and "colored" signs and emblems. Most historians agree that these laws not only separated the two races but by institutionalizing racial divisions they solidified the concept of superior versus inferior status. In essence, Jim Crow robbed African Americans of any voice in society. Historians Franklin and Moss summarize: "The law, the courts, the schools, and almost every institution in the South favored whites. This was white supremacy."[28]

Chapter Three

Life Under Jim Crow

As the twentieth century opened, the general outlook for African Americans under the Jim Crow system was not a bright one. Nearly 80 percent of African Americans in the South, in fact, lived under conditions that were little better than those that had existed under slavery. Their civil rights had been for the most part completely eliminated. Writing in 1903, African American novelist Charles W. Chesnutt addressed the situation: "The rights of the Negroes are at a lower ebb than at any time during the thirty-five years of their freedom, and the race prejudice is more intense and uncompromising."[29]

Pleas to the federal government for help went unanswered. John Roy Lynch of Mississippi, one of the few blacks who had managed to retain his seat in Congress in spite of Jim Crow, made an impassioned speech pleading with his colleagues to intercede on behalf of blacks: "If this unjust discrimination is to be longer tolerated by the American people . . . then I can only say with sorrow and regret that our boasted civilization is a fraud; our republican institutions a failure; our social system a disgrace; and our religion a complete hypocrisy."[30]

The impact of Jim Crow laws was widespread and never ending. From the schools to the trains, from the homes to the factories, African Americans were reminded that most of their fellow citizens believed them to be inferior and undeserving of equal treatment.

In this 1945 photo, a group of black men relax on the porch of a general store in Florida. A sign designates the store for blacks exclusively by order of the police.

African Americans survived as best they could, relying on the strength of their family values and turning inward to their communities and churches for support.

Jobs for African Americans

That support was critical, since there were few opportunities for African Americans to better themselves economically and socially. Many Southern states prohibited blacks from entering such professions as law or medicine. As a rule, only low-paying jobs such as farmhand, servant, or janitor were available to blacks. African American journalist Carl T. Rowan grew up in Tennessee and writes of his teenage years during the late 1930s: "I had mowed lawns, swept basements, unloaded boxcars of coal, dug basements, hoed bulb-grass out of lawns, and done scores of other menial tasks that fell to Negroes by default."[31] Young African American men, as they matured and sought to marry and begin families of their own, had to take any job that was offered them.

Thousands of African Americans, unable to find other work, accepted positions as servants in the homes of whites. Blacks held many positions within white households, from that of chauffeur to that of the children's nanny and nursemaid. Black domestic workers were well aware of their status in the family and knew without having to be told how they should behave while in the white home. Servants, for instance, always entered the house by the back door, drank out of separate water containers, and never conversed with their white employers unless spoken to first. Women, regardless of their real names, were called "cook," "nanny," "nurse," or even "nigger." Women servants, in particular, worked long hours. Historian Leon F. Litwack describes their day: "Up at dawn to prepare breakfast for the white family, cleaning the house in the morning, preparing lunch, washing clothes, making dinner . . . most black women worked a long day, often until ten o'clock at night." [32] These same women then returned home to care for their own children and maintain their own households.

An African American maid irons clothes in the kitchen of a white household. Large numbers of blacks were forced to accept menial positions in white homes.

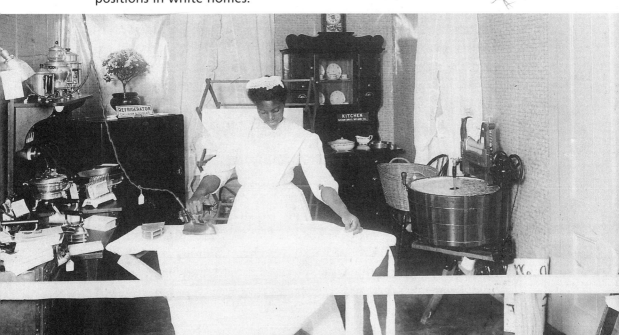

With jobs so few and so poorly paid, many African Americans created their own businesses, but few were able to achieve real success. Black entrepreneurs faced many obstacles in setting up these businesses. It was, for example, next to impossible for a black man to obtain a loan from a white-owned bank, while local and state business regulations discriminated against African American ownership by imposing high taxes, curtailing the choice of locations, and requiring compliance with impossibly restrictive building codes.

Despite these barriers a handful of black would-be entrepreneurs were able to succeed in fields where there was little to no white competition. These African American businessmen were actually able to turn the Jim Crow laws to their advantage. Such was the case in the field of barbering. Because white barbershops refused to serve black customers, African American barbers thrived by offering their services in black neighborhoods. A small number of African Americans also found success by opening banks and insurance companies that served other blacks. These establishments offered small business and home loans and insured both individuals and businesses when white-owned companies refused to do so. Another field open to African Americans was the funeral industry. With white mortuaries refusing to serve the black community, African American funeral homes flourished.

A handful of African Americans became wealthy businessmen. A.F. Herndon, for instance, became the wealthiest black in Atlanta. He operated the area's largest barbershop, served as president of an insurance company, and owned fifty houses that he rented out to other blacks. Such success stories, however, were rare, leaving most African Americans scrambling for any work they could find.

Sharecropping

That work, for the vast majority of African Americans during the latter part of the nineteenth century and early part of the twentieth century, consisted of what they had done most of their lives: farming. Hundreds of thousands of blacks became sharecroppers who worked on land that belonged to white planters. In exchange for the bulk of the profits, white planters provided the land, a place to live, livestock, seed, and the necessary farm equipment for their black employees.

Black customers get haircuts in a black-owned barbershop in New York City. Some black entrepreneurs managed to establish successful businesses under Jim Crow.

Black sharecroppers worked the land and then turned over the harvest to the planters, who were responsible for selling the crops. African Americans were given anywhere from one-fourth to one-third of the proceeds from the sale of the crop. Out of this money, however, the sharecroppers then had to pay for any food or supplies they had purchased from the planter—often at inflated prices. What this generally meant was that African Americans got no cash, or even worse, because of high interest rates charged by the planters, were deep in debt to their white employers. Hundreds of thousands of African American sharecroppers were thus deprived of their earnings. Goldfield elaborates: "There was no escape from the hard times, flimsy shacks, premature death, . . . and poverty that accompanied a life on the farm."[33]

Not only did sharecroppers earn little or no cash, but they worked long hours. Generally up before dawn, they worked twelve to sixteen

43

hours a day, plowing, planting, weeding, and harvesting crops such as cotton and tobacco. The entire African American family worked either in the fields or the home of the white landowner. Children, in addition to helping with the tilling and sowing of the land, also fed the livestock and did daily chores in the home. Elderly family members were responsible for growing small gardens of vegetables and helping preserve and store the produce. Despite the hard work and long hours, most sharecroppers were lucky if they earned enough to feed their families.

African American Housing

With income barely adequate to keep hunger at bay, anything beyond basic housing was simply unaffordable. The quality of housing for African Americans in the South and elsewhere was far below that available to whites. Even when a black family could afford a more

A sharecropper family sits on the porch of their shack in Arkansas. African American families typically lived in dilapidated shacks with no amenities.

Even at the Federal Level

■

With jobs few and far between, many African Americans sought employment with government agencies. Here, as in most segments of the job market, blacks were nearly always turned away. This was particularly true in the field of law enforcement. While a few blacks were hired as deputy sheriffs in the Far West, the majority of African Americans found strict segregation to be a fact of life.

Well into the twentieth century, even the Federal Bureau of Investigation practiced racial discrimination in hiring. African American lawyer and later Supreme Court justice Thurgood Marshall looked into the hiring policies of this organization in the early 1940s. He wrote a letter to then FBI director J. Edgar Hoover requesting statistics on the number of blacks employed in the agency. Hoover responded by assuring Marshall that there were dozens of black agents and field workers. Author Carl T. Rowan, in his book *Dream Makers, Dream Breakers: The World of Justice Thurgood Marshall,* describes the reality of the situation: "The truth was that the FBI had not a single black special agent, and put theater greasepaint on the faces of white agents when investigative work was required in all-black neighborhoods."

comfortable home, Jim Crow laws restricted their choice of location. Many communities specifically forbade African Americans from living in certain sections of town. Deeds were often written with clauses that prohibited their owners from selling to blacks unless the entire neighborhood approved. As a result, the majority of African Americans lived in cramped, old, dilapidated homes located in the least desirable sections of town.

These neighborhoods had few, if any, amenities. Streets were seldom paved, so during rainstorms they frequently turned into muddy quagmires. Most black neighborhoods lacked sewers and few homes had running water. These conditions greatly impacted the health of the black community, leading to increased rates of mortality and illness.

Even if there were no official restrictions on where blacks could live, the limits were still there. Lillian Smith, an African American writer, addresses these conditions in her 1949 autobiography *Killers of the Dream*. In talking about small towns of the South, she writes: "There are the invisible lines that turn and bend and cut the town into segments. Invisible, but electrically charged with taboo. Places you go, places you don't go. White town, colored town; white streets, colored streets; front door, back door. Places you sit. Places you cannot sit." [34]

The situation in the North for African Americans was no better. Rundown buildings, filth, rat-infested homes, no running water, lack of sanitation and heating, and high crime rates characterized these neighborhoods. As bad as the quality was, there was never enough housing, and as many as a dozen or more people were often forced to live in a house consisting of a single room. The residents of these areas were also victimized by white landlords who charged excessive rent and ignored the crumbling structures.

African American Health

Due in part to the poor housing conditions, African Americans suffered from a disproportionately large number of serious diseases, often deadly. The lack of municipal water supplies forced African Americans to rely on shallow wells for their drinking water, which was often contaminated with microorganisms that caused cholera and typhoid fever. Rain water collected in barrels also attracted mosquitoes that caused such diseases as malaria. Deaths from these diseases, along with tuberculosis, influenza, and measles, led to abnormally high mortality rates among the black population. According to the Atlanta Board of Health, in 1900 the African American death rate exceeded the white rate by nearly 70 percent. During this same time period nearly half of all black children in Atlanta died before their first birthday, usually from treatable and preventable childhood diseases.

White public health officials made efforts to explain these statistics by falling back on the stereotype of African Americans as inferior beings. For example, ignoring the lack of clean water supplies, politicians explained that African Americans had no particular concern for personal cleanliness. Whites throughout the South and elsewhere persuaded themselves that African Americans liked living in these kinds of conditions. Only when infectious diseases threatened to spread into white neighborhoods would local and state governments take action to improve conditions in African American sections of town.

Eventually, the federal government took a modest step toward improving the health of African Americans. In 1932 at the behest of black political activists and the growing concern of white communities regarding the spread of contagion, the U.S. Public Health Service created the Office of Negro Health. The members of this organization held a National Negro Health Week. During the seven-day period, millions of African American children were inoculated and entire black neighborhoods were cleaned up. The Office of Negro Health was instrumental in beginning the long, slow climb toward better health care for blacks by continuing the work begun during the 1930s and sponsoring periodic health weeks and other campaigns.

In Northern urban areas, African Americans typically lived in dank, filthy rooms (right) in run-down tenements like this one in New York City (left).

African American Youth

Growing up and living in such poor conditions and facing discrimination wherever they turned, every African American child had to learn to face the harsh reality of prospects that were limited at best. They knew from an early age, for instance, that their chances of receiving a quality education and living a prosperous life were limited. With limited job opportunities, African American youth understood that their futures would be filled with struggle and hardship.

Job Discrimination and the Great Migration

Trapped in an ever-increasing cycle of violence and poverty, thousands of African Americans chose to leave the South during the early twentieth century. Hearing of the need for workers in the North in World War I ammunition factories and other industries, entire families packed their meager belongings and headed north in the hope of finding employment and less discrimination. It has been estimated that during the 1910s over half a million African Americans migrated; while during the 1920s another seven hundred and fifty thousand made the trip north.

This Great Migration, as it is known to historians, gained impetus because of the booming World War I war economy in the Midwest and Northeast. Companies needed workers so badly that they were willing to hire African Americans. The largest year of the migration was 1916. Historians John Hope Franklin and Alfred A. Moss Jr. in their book *From Slavery to Freedom* explain: "The migration, coming when it did, gave blacks an opportunity for industrial development that they had never enjoyed before, and it relieved the labor shortage during the crucial years of the war."

Hundreds of thousands of African Americans found decent-paying jobs for the first time in their lives. Their success, however, was short-lived. When white American troops returned home after the war's end, the African Americans were fired and replaced with white workers. Once again, blacks found themselves unemployed and living in poverty.

Adding to these realizations was the understanding that these limitations were due solely to the color of their skin. Discrimination and segregation were a fact of life for black youth, and they understood from a very early age that they must live in accordance with Jim Crow or suffer the consequences. They realized, for instance, that they needed to contain their feelings of frustration lest they face violence and other repercussions from their white neighbors. They were also fully aware that in order to survive in the South they had to carefully weigh each word, gesture, and movement in the presence of whites.

These realizations only served to increase the humiliation and hopelessness young African Americans already felt about their living conditions. When young African Americans asked their parents why they had to live as they did, their parents usually responded with "Don't ask," or "That's just the way it is." African American youth grew up feeling powerless to do anything about their own predicament. They knew that if they wanted to survive in the South, they would have to learn the art of getting along with white Southerners. Any deviation, they knew, could result in violent or even deadly reprisal.

For many black youths early racial encounters became defining moments in their lives. These incidents, usually in the form of punishment or violence at the hands of whites, were instigated mostly by whites, the purpose being, according to historian Litwack, to "impress on a new generation the solidarity of racial lines and the unchallengeable authority and superiority of the dominant race."[35]

Accepting white supremacy, however, was unlikely to help them rise in the estimation of whites. Pauli Murray, author of *Proud Shoes: The Story of an American Family,* published in 1955, writes about what it was like growing up under Jim Crow:

> We were bottled up and labeled and set aside—sent to the Jim Crow car, the back of the bus, the sidedoor of the theater, the side window of a restaurant. We came to know that whatever we had was always inferior. We came to understand that no matter how neat and clean, how law-abiding, submissive, and polite, how studious in school, how churchgoing and moral, how scrupulous in paying our bills and taxes we were, it made no essential difference in our place.[36]

The African American Community

African Americans throughout the United States realized, therefore, that help in alleviating their plight would have to come from within the black community. Fairclough elaborates: "Hemmed in by walls of prejudice, blacks created havens of security within families, communities, and churches."[37]

In an effort to improve their lives in the early twentieth century, the African American community created a number of social organizations. The Conference on Negro Problems, for instance, began meeting in Atlanta in 1896 and every year thereafter until 1914 for the purpose of studying and developing possible solutions to problems. The group recommended, for example, that African Americans pursue educational and vocational opportunities. Their suggestions, while theoretically sound, effected only minor improvements and changes in the racial situation and the reality of African American life.

Of greater practical importance, during the Great Depression of the 1930s African Americans organized local groups to maximize their economic opportunities. The Colored Merchants Association of New York, for instance, bought food and other goods in large volumes at low prices and then distributed the items to the poor. This group also boycotted stores that had African American customers but failed to hire any black employees. Another association, the Jobs for Negroes Organization, was set up in New York City, Chicago, Cleveland, and St. Louis. The purpose of this group was to find jobs for African Americans by appealing to white employers to hire more blacks, a tactic that met with little success.

Other organizations also played an important role in the African American community. The National League on Urban Conditions Among Negroes, an organization that later became the National Urban League, helped African Americans adjust to life in northern cities. Another organization, the Colored Farmers Alliance, helped African American farmers earn higher prices for their goods by selling them collectively.

In a few cases the African American community joined with whites of good will to create programs and organizations that would benefit both races. The Commission on Interracial Cooperation, for instance, was formed in 1919. Founded by prominent white Southern ministers and social workers and a handful of black lead-

Mary McLeod Bethune

Mary McLeod Bethune was one of many African American women who became politically and socially active in the early twentieth century. She devoted her entire life to working to improve education for black children. Her dream, from the time she was a small child picking cotton in South Carolina, was to start a school for African American children.

After graduating from Moody Bible Institute, Bethune moved to Daytona Beach, Florida, where she built and opened the Daytona Educational and Industrial Training School for Negro Girls. As the enrollment in the school increased, Bethune opened a boardinghouse in her home for the students. She baked cookies and cakes and staged many public choir concerts to raise money to improve the school. With the help of white northern benefactors, Bethune was able to build a larger school and began accepting male students. In 1923 Bethune's school merged with Cookman Institute in Jacksonville, Florida, and became Bethune-Cookman College, a fully accredited liberal arts institution of higher learning.

Bethune's determination to improve African American life did not end with the establishment of this college. In 1935 Bethune founded the National Council of Negro Women and dedicated herself to working for equal rights and opportunities for African Americans. She continued to remain politically and socially active, serving in both the Roosevelt and Truman administrations. Throughout her life she was a strong and vocal voice speaking out on behalf of African Americans of all ages.

In this photo from the 1940s, Mary McLeod Bethune stands with a group of students in front of Bethune-Cookman College in Florida.

ers, the commission set up a program of education that addressed racial relations at the state and local level in the South. It offered a ten-day course that would train black and white leaders to do interracial work. The commission's goal was not to challenge the Jim Crow system but merely to ameliorate its harshest effects. Thus, the success of this training program was that it did criticize discrimination; the downfall of the group, however, was that it failed to attack segregation.

The Role of African American Women

No one played a more significant role in the African American community than black women. Living in poverty and with their husbands shut out of jobs, it fell upon African American women to hold their families together—often both emotionally and financially.

A preacher delivers a spirited sermon to his black congregation. Throughout the Jim Crow era, the church served as a place of refuge for the black community.

They did this by seeking work as domestic servants in the homes of wealthy whites. These jobs provided much-needed income that enabled their families to survive during times when their husbands were out of work. Despite working full-time jobs, black women also provided love, encouragement, and support to family members.

In addition to providing emotional and financial support to their families, black women also created networks of friends and family to support one another, and participated in their churches and mutual aid groups. African American women joined social clubs and had great success in making differences within their own communities. In an immense scope of activities, African American clubwomen founded schools, orphanages, clinics, hospitals, homes for the elderly, and hostels for single women. They ran kindergartens and mounted public health campaigns. These efforts, while having little effect on the Jim Crow system, provided material support to thousands of African American communities. A few also became politically active, forming the National Association of Colored Women in 1896. This organization provided a forum for the views of African American women across the United States and was instrumental in setting up girls' homes and hospitals throughout the South.

Black women also played a crucial role in black churches. Within congregations women taught in church schools, held fund-raisers, cleaned buildings, prepared suppers, and ran social service networks. They also ministered to the sick and needy. African American women demanded and received very public roles within their churches, often playing an important role in the hiring and firing of ministers and the selection of subjects taught in schools.

The Role of African American Churches

With black women playing important roles, African American churches provided the black community with support and a refuge during the Jim Crow era. The end of the Civil War had seen an expansion in the membership of independent African American churches. Thousands of blacks began withdrawing from white churches and found welcoming homes in the burgeoning memberships of black churches. Barred from most areas of social and political life in the United States, hundreds of thousands of African Americans turned more and more to the church for support and hope.

In addition to its religious function, the church served as a school, a lecture hall, a social and recreational center, a meeting place for an assortment of groups, and a source of information. African American ministers were very influential members of society. Litwack elaborates: "Perhaps the most positive role the minister might play in a time of retreat, violence, and repression was to instill in his people the spiritual resources that would enable them to survive." [38]

African American church leaders, around the turn of the century, also began to speak out against discrimination. The Colored Methodist Bishops, for instance, made an appeal to white Americans in 1908 that stated: "We appeal to the friends of humanity to use their influence to rid this glorious country of mob violence which is sending so many to an untimely grave. . . . We appeal to the liberty loving men in authority to lend us their assistance by influence, by legislation for the removal of the Jim Crow . . . laws." [39]

Despite these individual and group efforts, African American life changed little in the first half of the twentieth century. The Jim Crow system was firmly entrenched throughout the country, effectively discriminating against blacks in every aspect of life and keeping African Americans segregated and downtrodden economically. White supremacy maintained a strong hold on society throughout the United States and, particularly in the South, whites were prepared to use extreme measures to maintain that hold.

Chapter Four

Violence and Injustice

The pervasiveness and effectiveness of the Jim Crow system was made possible primarily through fear, engendered by beatings, arson, and murder. Violence, in fact, was so widespread during the late nineteenth and early twentieth centuries that no African American family was spared. Dray addresses the legacy of this violence: "It is a living memory to most black Americans that their forbears were lynched and routinely subjected to violence and intimidation, and that they lived in almost constant fear of seeing a loved one lynched or of being targeted themselves."[40]

Everyday Violence

During the years of Reconstruction, violence had been used to keep the freed slaves from exercising their newly granted civil rights. White Southerners, in their attempt to maintain white supremacy, wanted to keep African Americans in a subservient position. Violence, in many cases, was not designed to punish alleged offenders but rather to send a message to the entire black community. The message was simple: Whites were in charge and blacks were vulnerable; therefore, it was futile to try to change things.

By the late nineteenth century a new generation of African Americans had been born into freedom. Through hard work some members of this generation achieved success in the field of business and

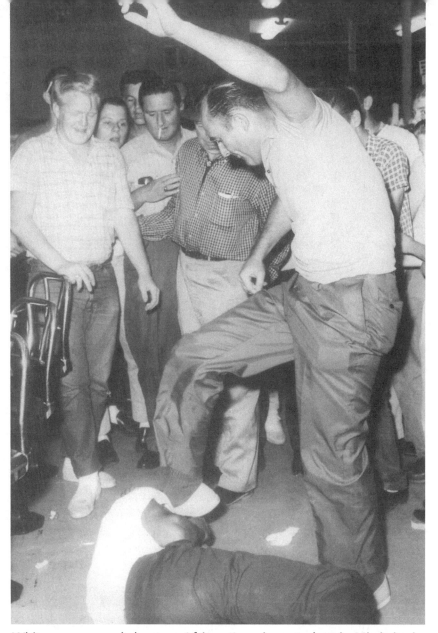

White men savagely beat an African American student in Mississippi. White Southerners routinely resorted to violence as a means to keep blacks from exercising their civil rights.

other endeavors. White Southerners greatly feared this new generation and the success and influence they acquired within the black community. Fearing that these black individuals would continue to prosper and perhaps aspire to equality, whites throughout the South were determined to silence them and prevent them from challenging the racial status quo. Thus, some of the most frequent targets of violence during the Jim Crow years became those African Americans who had been successful in gaining an education, forming a business, or earning a profit from the land.

Many blacks were beaten and then run off their land simply so whites could obtain their property. African American farmers reported numerous incidents in which their tools were damaged or stolen, their mules poisoned, and their crops destroyed. In many parts of the South, whites posted signs near blacks' farms: "If you have not moved away by sundown tomorrow, we will shoot you like rabbits."[41] Fearing violence, thousands of black farmers abandoned their land and fled the South. Once the blacks had vacated the land, it was a simple matter for whites to take ownership by merely moving there and filing a claim for ownership.

Sometimes African Americans found themselves targeted even when it was clear that they were just passing through a Southern town. Black soldiers, traveling while on leave, for example, were often victimized. The reasons behind this victimization lay in the fact that many African American soldiers came home from overseas wanting to fight discrimination. After having enjoyed the respectful manner in which they were treated in Europe, black veterans pledged to work to gain the same respect at home. With blacks no longer willing to accept second-class citizenship, the very sight of a black soldier in uniform enraged white Southerners to the point of violence. Isaac Woodward, for example, upon his discharge from the military, took a bus from Georgia to his home in New York City. Just across the South Carolina border Woodward and the bus driver quarreled about Woodward taking too long in the bathroom at a rest stop. The driver radioed ahead to authorities in Batesburg, South Carolina. There Woodward was ordered off the bus and taken by police chief Linwood Shull and a deputy into an alley where the two white men beat the black soldier almost to death. One of them shoved a blunt club into Woodward's eyes, permanently blinding him.

Incidents such as this were common throughout the United States during the Jim Crow era. African Americans were subjected to intimidation and violence on a near daily basis. No black family was unaffected. Blacks were insulted, kicked, beaten, and arrested for daring to interact with whites, for using segregated facilities, or for appearing to be disrespectful to white women.

The Perpetrators

The white perpetrators of violence against blacks came from all walks of life and from all age groups. White youths frequently attacked black children while on the way to school, while older white Southerners participated in acts of arson and violence against black businessmen, teachers, and ministers. Among the worst perpetrators of violence during the Jim Crow years, however, were members of white supremacist groups such as the Ku Klux Klan.

The Klan, originally formed in the early years of Reconstruction, had played a key role in preventing blacks from exercising their rights in the late nineteenth century. They had accomplished this through the use of threats, intimidation, and actual acts of violence against black individuals and black communities. Wearing long, flowing white robes and conical hats to disguise their appearance, the Klan terrorized hundreds of thousands of African Americans.

The Klan, with its membership reaching 4 million in the 1920s, continued to play a significant role in the perpetration of racial violence in the early years of the twentieth century. They burned black schools, churches, and homes and administered beatings to black businessmen, black landowners, and educated blacks. African Americans were beaten for refusing to work with whites, for having jobs that whites wanted, for reading a newspaper or having books in their homes, and for opening businesses. Often simply beating someone was not enough—Klan members resorted to murder, often in the form of lynching.

Lynching

It was, in fact, lynching that ultimately became the symbol of the efforts to maintain white supremacy in the South. In addition to hanging, lynching included humiliation, torture, burning, dismemberment, beating, whipping, shooting, and castration. The issue of a person's guilt was secondary, since the mob served as prosecutor, judge, jury, and executioner. Hundreds of innocent black men, suspected of some crime, were captured by white mobs, taken to the woods, beaten, and then killed without ever having been arrested, tried, or found guilty of any crime.

During the Jim Crow era thousands of blacks were killed by lynch mobs. The actual number of African Americans who were lynched is unknown, although most historians agree that the number reaches

The Twentieth-Century Ku Klux Klan

Briefly disbanded in the 1870s, the Ku Klux Klan (KKK) experienced a resurgence of popularity in 1915 and boosted its national membership into the millions. Still relying on secrecy and disguise, its members attacked not only African Americans, but Jews, Catholics, immigrants, homosexuals, and Communists. These targets were selected, according to Klan bylaws, for the purpose of maintaining the purity of America. This group, like its predecessors, used fear and violence to terrorize black neighborhoods and was responsible for thousands of African American and other deaths. This group, unlike the earlier Klan, burned crosses as a symbol of their intent to terrorize.

The Klan of the early twentieth century never totally disbanded and was resurrected yet again during the 1950s as the civil rights movement was getting underway. Primarily Southern in membership, the KKK reached its peak membership in the 1960s and targeted primarily African Americans. The Klan played a visible role in the burning of black churches throughout the South and was responsible for thousands of crimes, including the murder of numerous civil rights workers who were working on black voter registration in the South. Few of the perpetrators were ever punished. The modern Klan is small in membership and fragmented, but maintains cells known as klaverns scattered throughout the United States.

Members of the Ku Klux Klan show the strength of their numbers in a 1925 march in Washington, D.C.

into the tens of thousands. This number is deceptively low as the majority of lynchings and killings were never reported. The highest number of fatalities occurred between 1882 and 1927, with over 95 percent of the victims being killed in the South. It is estimated that during those years whites shot and lynched blacks at an average of at least one every two and a half days.

White Southerners believed that lynching was the best method to defend white domination. "Lynching became almost a necessary

Rape as a Justification for Violence

White Southerners used the myth of black men as sexual predators to justify countless lynchings. African American orator and abolitionist Frederick Douglass addressed this issue in the late nineteenth century. Author William S. McFeely, in his biography of Douglass, repeats the orator's words: "An abandoned woman has only to start the cry that she had been insulted by a black man to have him arrested and summarily murdered by the mob." Only swift, certain, and terrible punishment, whites argued, could prevent the rape of white women by black men from reaching epidemic proportions.

The statistics, however, do not support such a claim and, in fact, bear out the reality that very few white women were actual-

ly attacked by black men. The facts, however, did not stop white Southerners from utilizing the myth to justify their violent actions. Hundreds of African American men, unjustly accused of rape, were brutalized and murdered during the years of Jim Crow.

In 1935 these young black men were lynched by an angry white mob in Mississippi after they were accused of raping a white woman.

practice," one historian asserts, "that served to give dramatic warning to all black inhabitants that the ironclad system of white supremacy was not to be challenged by deed, word, or even gesture."[42] As a result, the lynch mob became the most feared symbol of white supremacy.

African Americans were lynched for the smallest of crimes and, in many cases, for no reason at all. Blacks were killed for registering to vote, arguing with white men, loitering, drunkenness, refusing to step aside, and disorderly conduct. Litwack elaborates further: "All too often, black Southerners, innocent of any crime or offense, were victims of lynchings or burnings because they were black and in the wrong place at the wrong time. For some [whites] 'nigger killing' had simply become a sport."[43]

White Southerners believed that lynching was necessary to keep African Americans in their place. One white Southerner confirmed this by stating: "It is about time to have another lynching. When the niggers get so that they are not afraid of being lynched, it is time to put the fear in them."[44] Lynching was thus seen as a necessary tool so that new generations of African Americans knew their "place" in Southern society.

The Anatomy of a Lynching

From the moment the first African slave arrived on American shores blacks had faced violence and death at the hands of white Americans. Despite this fact, the killings that occurred during the Jim Crow era differed in many respects from earlier deaths. Litwack explains why the lynchings of the late nineteenth and early twentieth centuries were so different:

"What was strikingly new and different . . . was the sadism and exhibitionism that characterized white violence. . . . To kill the victim was not enough; the execution needed to be turned into a public ritual, a collective experience, and the victim needed to be subjected to extraordinary torture and mutilation."[45]

Historians say that one of the most bizarre characteristics of Jim Crow lynching was the presence of thousands of spectators. White men, women, and children throughout the South frequently dressed in their Sunday best to attend the well-publicized lynchings of African Americans. People came from hundreds of miles around to view the killings. For instance, in 1893 Henry Smith, an innocent black man, was captured and arrested for the murder of a local policeman in a small Texas town. Already convicted of the crime in the minds of townspeople, the local newspapers, with the complicity of the sheriff's office, announced the intention to execute Smith at the hands of a lynch mob. So many residents of Texas and neighboring Arkansas wanted to see Smith executed that special excursion trains were chartered, while schools let children out for the day so they could attend. Smith was placed on a carnival float, paraded through town, and then taken to a scaffold where the victim's family thrust hot irons onto his body. His body was covered with oil and then set on fire to the cheers of the spectators.

Grace Elizabeth Hale describes the carnival atmosphere of many lynchings: "Lynchers drove cars, spectators used cameras, out-of-town visitors arrived on specially chartered excursion trains, and the towns and counties in which these horrifying events happened had newspapers, telegraph offices, and even radio stations that announced times and locations of these upcoming violent spectacles."[46] When eighteen-year-old Jesse Washington was lynched in Waco, Texas, an estimated fifteen thousand whites watched and cheered.

Another macabre part of the "lynching experience" was the taking of souvenirs. Pieces of the body, including bone fragments, were prized possessions for many whites throughout the South. Dray elaborates: "The experience of having witnessed the event was thought by many incomplete if one did not go home with some piece of cooked human being."[47]

Red Summer

In addition to lynching and murder, there were numerous other forms of violence that were perpetrated against African Americans during the Jim Crow era. In the decade after World War I a pattern of racial violence emerged that was characterized by riots and mob assaults against entire African American communities. Many historians refer to these occurrences not as riots but as massacres and mass lynchings. Large-scale interracial violence became nearly epidemic.

During the summer and fall of 1919 there were twenty-six riots nationwide as violence erupted in both the North and the South. Franklin and Moss elaborate: "It was the nation's worst race war

In Tulsa, Oklahoma, during the early summer of 1921, even more radical techniques were employed. Historian Robert A. Gibson describes the situation: "Machine guns were brought into use; eight airplanes were employed to spy on the movements of the Negroes and, according to some, were used in bombing the colored section."[50] The severity of the technique was defended by whites as a necessary means of keeping blacks in their place.

The Role of the Police

Members of lynch mobs and white rioters were rarely if ever brought to justice. If there were any investigation of any of the deaths of blacks at all, the finding was usually "death by parties unknown." The matter would then simply be dropped. Prior to 1930, of the tens of thousands of people who participated in the murder of African Americans, fewer than fifty were indicted nationwide and only four were sentenced to jail. In many cases the white perpetrators not only escaped punishment but were praised by the legal authorities and in local newspaper editorials for their actions. The papers printed frequent condemnations of residents of black neighborhoods while at the same time applauding the efforts of whites to rid cities of what were called "undesirable elements."

Far from preventing violence against blacks, Southern police officers played a large and visible role as the enforcers of white supremacy by harassing African Americans, arresting them without cause, and turning the other way when white mobs took matters into their own hands. Joseph Boskin, the author of *Urban Racial Violence,* focused on the role of the police in not stopping or punishing white violence. Boskin writes: "The police force, more than any other institution, was invariably involved as a precipitating cause or perpetuating factor in the riots. In almost every one of the riots the police sided with the attackers, either by participating in, or by failing to quell the attack."[51]

In addition to their abetting the violence committed by others, white police forces also used excessive force in their questioning of African Americans and during their patrols of black neighborhoods. This force, historians contend, was meant to remind African Americans of their inferior place in society. Litwack elaborates on this concept: Police operated on the principle, he writes, "that blacks understood only force, that they worked and behaved best under the threat of the lash, and their uncontrolled impulses required a special quality of discipline."[52]

Injustice for African Americans

If whites were rarely prosecuted for crimes against blacks, the same could not be said when the accused was African American. Equal justice remained elusive for African Americans throughout the country and especially in the South during the entire Jim Crow era. Litwack explains how justice often was denied to African Americans: "Verdicts were based less on evidence of guilt than on the race of the defendant and the deeply rooted assumption that black men and women were by nature more prone to criminality and impulsive violence than whites and required more rigid control and restraint."[53] Minor crimes committed by African Americans, such as petty theft and drunkenness, were treated severely by white judges, who sentenced those convicted to long prison terms. By contrast, when whites were accused of these same crimes, they were usually acquitted or released after a brief stay in jail.

When a crime was committed against an African American, justice was also in short supply. To even bring charges against a white person could result in violence and often death. In Mississippi, for instance, a judge ruled that there was no law that allowed the courts to punish a white man for beating an African American. And in Maryland a judge ruled that it was an insult to ask a white man to apologize to any black. Moreover, even when there were abundant black witnesses to a crime committed by a white person, the court often disallowed black testimony and moved to a quick dismissal of all charges.

In most trials of African Americans, the outcome was a foregone conclusion. Defendants' testimony and that of supportive witnesses were usually disregarded. Since the majority of white attorneys refused to represent blacks and African American lawyers were scarce (most law schools refused to admit blacks), defendants were often left without legal representation in court. Even when an African American attorney was available, Jim Crow rules often meant that he or she had to sit and argue the case from an upstairs gallery. White witnesses would frequently refuse to answer black lawyers' questions, and judges would do nothing to force cooperation. Few trials lasted more than a few hours, and in many cases the sentences were handed down so quickly that an African American defendant could not even enter a plea for mercy.

In any event, no matter what the sentence, a lynch mob was often ready to take matters into its own hands. Only rarely were law enforcement personnel expected to protect their prisoners. By the early 1900s Alabama and the non–Jim Crow state of Indiana had a system for fining sheriffs who failed to protect their prisoners. Seldom, however, were there any substantial fines actually imposed. Only in rare cases did anyone intervene on behalf of jailed African Americans. One such incident occurred in Carroll County, Tennessee, although it was the wife of Sheriff. J.C. Butler who took it upon her-

In the Jim Crow era some states had laws requiring law enforcement officers to protect their prisoners. They were seldom enforced.

self to defy a lynch mob that had arrived at the jail during her husband's absence. Mrs. Butler, with a shotgun in her hands, addressed the crowd: "If you come in here it will be over my dead body. You can shoot me down if you will, but you can't have my prisoner."[54]

An antilynching law had also been passed in Illinois thanks in part to the efforts of outspoken African American writer Ida B. Wells. The law called for the removal of any sheriff who failed to do all he could to protect a prisoner. The law was tested in 1909 after the Cairo, Illinois, sheriff told a lynch mob where his pris-

Ida B. Wells

Ida B. Wells, one of the best-known African American political activists of the Jim Crow era, was born into slavery during the Civil War. After attending school, she ultimately moved to Memphis, Tennessee, where she became the editor of a local newspaper called the *Evening Star* and began writing articles describing segregation and discrimination. Her articles were reprinted in numerous African American papers throughout the United States.

Wells's attention was turned toward lynching following the murder of her close friend Thomas Moss in 1892. She began writing articles and pamphlets describing the horrors of lynching and appealing to the American public to correct the wrongs that were being done. She ultimately became one of the world's first investigative reporters when she set out to gather facts and figures by interviewing victims' families.

Eventually Wells traveled to England to spread her ideas. Historian Philip Dray in his book *At the Hand of Persons Unknown: The Lynching of Black America* summarizes her intentions: "To Wells, such exposure could be invaluable because the American press largely accepted the Southern fable that lynchings resulted from the actions of black rapists." Her English audiences were appalled when Wells began to describe the evils of lynching. For the first time, the American press was forced to reconsider their attitudes. Wells insisted that whites were the problem and that African Americans were the victims and those in need of compassion and justice. Until her death in 1931 she remained one of the most persistent African American voices for justice and equality.

oner, a black man charged (unfairly) with murder, was being held. The man was ultimately taken by the mob and killed. The sheriff was removed from his position and Wells herself appeared before the governor of Illinois, Charles S. Deneen, pleading with him not to order his reinstatement. Deneen later shocked the nation by granting Wells's request. This courageous act on the governor's part sent a powerful message and helped end lynching in Illinois.

African American Response

Such responses from white authorities were the exception, however. For the most part, African Americans were helpless in the face of injustice and violence. Occasionally, blacks fought back—using stones, bricks, and on occasion guns—but black armed resistance was usually futile and led to more lynchings and violence. Litwack explains: "Black uprisings were mostly spontaneous, unorganized, individualistic, and quickly and ruthlessly suppressed."[55]

Still, African Americans tried to speak out about the situation they faced. Black newspapers were among the first to take a stand against the violence and murder. The *Detroit Plain Dealer* in the late nineteenth century pleaded with the nation to be aware of what was happening: "All over this country, the people should be aroused, meetings held, organizations formed, and offers of assistance in a substantial way be made to bring these murderers to justice."[56] African American editors in the South paid a high price, however, for expressing their outrage. Often, newspapers' offices would be burned and their editors killed or jailed.

African American women were particularly vocal in expressing their outrage at the lynchings and murders. Long before she confronted the governor of Illinois, Ida B. Wells had taken the forefront in the fight against lynching. In 1892 she published a pamphlet titled *Southern Horrors, Lynch Law in All Its Phases*, describing the killings in graphic terms. She spoke out frequently about the murders being committed. In an 1892 speech she stated:

> So bold have the lynchers become masks are laid aside, the temples of justice and strongholds of law are invaded in broad daylight, and prisoners taken out and lynched while governors of states and officers of law stand by. . . . And yet the Christian nation . . . says it can do nothing to stop this

Members of the NAACP march with antilynching placards in Washington, D.C., in 1934. That year an antilynching bill died in the Senate.

inhuman slaughter. . . . I think it is high time the justice-loving and law-abiding people should take some steps to make such acts impossible. [57]

Wells's efforts, along with those of other leading reformers, eventually helped persuade Congress to consider antilynching legislation in the early 1920s. Leonidas C. Dyer, a representative from Missouri, introduced a bill specifically outlawing lynching. The bill passed the House of Representatives by a vote of 231 to 119 in early January 1922 but died in the Senate as Southern senators impeded its passage through long speeches and other delaying tactics. A later bill met a similar fate in 1934. No law specifically outlawing lynching was ever passed by the U.S. Congress. Only by continuing to speak out against the horrors of lynching were black leaders eventually able to rouse the nation's conscience and gradually end the violence.

Chapter Five

Accommodation or Protest: Responding to Jim Crow

During the Jim Crow era African Americans in the South had limited choices in their response to white supremacy, violence, and the discrimination they suffered in their everyday lives. One option was to flee, and hundreds of thousands of African Americans chose to migrate westward or northward in search of racial equality and improved living conditions. Those who stayed in the South had two other choices—either to learn to live with segregation or fight against it by any means at their disposal.

In the late nineteenth century each alternative found a champion within the leadership of the black community. While both leaders had as their ultimate goal equality for African Americans, the means they advocated were very different. On one hand, Booker T. Washington urged blacks to live with segregation and make accommodations to whites in the hope of better treatment in the future. On the other hand, W.E.B. DuBois advocated resistance to Jim Crow in the form of protests and legal action. These two leaders and their views contended for dominance among African Americans for the first two decades of the twentieth century.

A Gap in Leadership

Washington's call for accommodation was something of a change from what black leaders had been saying during the first thirty years after the end of the Civil War. During this time African American leaders had focused on speaking out against the evils of lynching and attempting to sway the American public in their fight for equality. Most prominent among these leaders was Frederick Douglass, who prior to the Civil War had been the leading spokesman for African American emancipation. After the Civil War, Douglass had continued to champion African American rights. Appearing frequently at public lectures, he spoke eloquently of the need for an end to discrimination and lynching. For example, in a speech in Elmira, New York, on August 1, 1880, Douglass spoke of the discrimination he saw everywhere he traveled:

> Today, in most of the Southern states, the Fourteenth and Fifteenth Amendments are virtually nullified. The rights which they were intended to guarantee are denied and held in contempt. The citizenship granted in the Fourteenth Amendment is practically a mockery, and the right to vote . . . is literally stamped out in the face of government. The old master class is today triumphant, and the newly enfranchised class is in a condition but little above that in which they were found before the rebellion. [58]

The Emergence of Booker T. Washington

After Douglass's death Washington was the first African American to emerge as a contender for leadership among African Americans. Washington, a former slave, believed that blacks should concentrate on economic advancement and urged African Americans to stop demanding political power and social equality. He also asked whites to help blacks gain an education and make a decent living. Washington's idea was that African Americans should accept segregation for the time being while working to gain acceptance by whites through hard work and thriftiness.

Washington believed that economic advancement could only come if blacks were provided with marketable skills. He used his school,

Tuskegee Normal and Industrial Institute, as a prime example of what African Americans could achieve with the proper training. This Alabama school, which Washington had founded in 1881, offered African Americans an opportunity to learn skills such as carpentry, farming, and mechanics. Fairclough elaborates on the importance of the

Frederick Douglass was a tireless champion of African American rights in the years following the Civil War. He is pictured here addressing a group of sympathetic whites.

Booker T. Washington (front row, third from left) poses with philanthropist Andrew Carnegie (on Washington's left) and the faculty of the Tuskegee Institute.

school: "To black people in America, and to black Africans and West Indies as well, Tuskegee was a proud symbol of what their race could achieve. It was a beacon of hope."[59]

The work that Washington had done through his school and his speeches made him a role model for hundreds of thousands of African Americans. The black community saw in Washington a successful black man who had made a name and positive reputation for himself. For many, Washington was an example of what could be achieved through hard work and diligence.

Policy of Accommodation

Washington's ideas also appealed to Southern white leaders, who invited him to address the Atlanta Cotton States and International Exposition, on September 18, 1895. Calling on African Americans to work within the existing conditions in the South, Washington criticized black protest against segregation. He emphasized that, while African Americans should not be deprived of the vote by unfair means, political agitation alone would not serve the interests of blacks. He stressed instead the role of hard work and character in advancing the cause of black equality throughout the United States.

Washington had long believed that if African Americans worked hard and showed their willingness to do what whites demanded, whites would learn over time to respect them. In his autobiography, *Up from Slavery,* he wrote: "I think that the whole future of my race hinges on the question as to whether or not it can make itself of such indispensable value that the people in the town and the state where we reside will feel that our presence is necessary to the happiness and well-being of the community." [60]

Washington's speech and his stated opinion that African Americans were not fully prepared to exercise their political rights were well received by the white community. His words at the exposition comprised what historians refer to as the Atlanta Compromise, an informal and unwritten pledge that Washington, as a nationally recognized leader of the black community, would not push for political equality for blacks. White Southerners were overwhelmingly pleased to hear a black leader urge accommodation and not protest. Washington, by making these statements, was actually supporting many of the same arguments that whites had made for decades. Dray elaborates on the meaning of the compromise: "In exchange for being given the chance to work and prove themselves, blacks would relinquish immediate demands for political and social equality." [61]

Opposition to Accommodation

Washington's Atlanta Compromise, however, was not universally accepted within the African American community. In particular, black intellectuals said the so-called compromise was not a compromise at all. Blacks had made all the concessions, they argued, while whites gave nothing in return. Many prominent African Americans perceived Washington's strategy as a virtual acceptance of the Jim Crow system. DuBois, who was emerging as a leading voice among African Americans, charged that "the Washington program . . . [is] a tacit acceptance of the alleged inferiority of the Negro." [62] DuBois, along with other black leaders, believed that by deferring to Southern whites African Americans would only guarantee that discrimination and segregation would continue.

Other African Americans were incensed with a claim Washington had made—that life had improved for blacks. Fairclough addresses some of their concerns: "The gains blacks made through education and self-help could not compensate for Jim Crow laws, disenfranchisement, lynching, employment discrimination, and manifold other oppressions."[63] In failing to denounce lynching and segregation, African American writers and leaders asserted, Washington had failed to grasp the reality of life in the South. In the years that followed, it became painfully clear to African Americans that accommodation had done little to end racial discrimination.

The Rise of W.E.B. DuBois

DuBois was particularly outspoken in his criticism of accommodation. In 1905 DuBois convened a group of nearly thirty fellow black intellectuals, the goal being to draw up a list of demands that, if implemented, would have granted African Americans full civil rights. Forced to meet in Canada because appropriate hotels in the United States refused to accommodate blacks, this group came to be known as the Niagara Movement, after the name of the town where they gathered, Niagara Falls, Ontario. Led by the charismatic DuBois, the group, according to Franklin and Moss, "demanded freedom of speech and criticism, male suffrage, the abolition of all distinctions based on race, the recognition of the basic principles of human fellowship, and respect for the working person."[64] The Niagara Movement called for improvements in educational facilities and an end to segregation, racial violence, and disenfranchisement. Indeed, the Niagara Movement called for the elimination of all social distinctions based on race.

The Niagara Movement's message roused in many African Americans a sense that something needed to be done to fight segregation, although no mass demonstrations resulted. Nor did the Niagara Movement have any real impact in the South. DuBois and other leaders of the Niagara Movement failed to develop a strategy for translating their words into action. Financing never materialized, and by 1910, the Niagara Movement had disbanded. The movement did, however, set the stage for the emergence of a bigger and more powerful organization.

In 1905 W.E.B. DuBois organized the Niagara Movement, a group of intellectuals that worked to improve the lives of blacks in the United States.

The Founding of the NAACP

The larger organization began taking shape even before the Niagara Movement had completely vanished. In 1909 a group of white social reformers, concerned over what they saw as a deteriorating racial situation, called a conference to see what might be done. An invitation was sent out that read: "We call upon all believers in democracy to join in a national conference for the discussion of present evils, the voicing of protests, and the renewal of the struggle for civil and political liberty."[65] Among those invited were DuBois, Wells, and other African American leaders.

As a result of this conference, the National Association for the Advancement of Colored People (NAACP) came into being.

The Back-to-Africa Movement

An alternative to either accommodation or protest was the back-to-Africa movement. The best-known proponent of a return to Africa was Marcus Garvey, a Jamaican immigrant who believed that whites would never accept African Americans as equals. He totally rejected the idea that blacks would ever be integrated into American society, suggesting instead that African Americans find pride in their race and return to Africa, their ancestral homeland.

Garvey's ideas were enthusiastically endorsed by hundreds of thousands of African Americans, primarily those who lived in the ghettos of the North. Despairing of their lives ever improving, poor blacks found in Garvey's words something positive to dream about. Historian Adam Fairclough, in his book *Better Day Coming: Blacks and Equality, 1890–2000,* wrote of Garvey's appeal: "Garvey gave black Americans something they had never before felt so clearly and unequivocally: the sense that they were a people—a nation—with a proud past, a heroic present, and a magnificent future."

To provide transport for those African Americans who wanted to go to Africa, Garvey founded a steamship company called the Black Star Line. Declaring himself the provisional president of Africa, Garvey's ambitions grew and he became increasingly autocratic. Eventually, however, Garvey suffered a series of setbacks. The collapse of the Black Star Line led to Garvey's conviction on charges of fraud, effectively ending his back-to-Africa movement.

Black emigrants in Georgia board a ship bound for Liberia as part of the back-to-Africa movement.

According to its constitution, the NAACP was founded "to achieve, through peaceful and lawful means, equal citizenship rights for all American citizens by eliminating segregation and discrimination in housing, employment, voting, schools, the courts, transportation, and recreation."[66] In many ways the NAACP represented the culmination of DuBois's position of resistance rather than accommodation. The organization pledged to fight, through the legal system, for equality and an end to discrimination. By 1920 the organization had over ninety thousand members in 356 different local branches.

Impact of the NAACP

The new organization succeeded where the Niagara Movement had failed. By sponsoring public meetings and offering legal challenges to Jim Crow, the NAACP challenged white supremacy in the South and elsewhere. Whites throughout the country, however, were not prepared to tolerate an organization that openly challenged racial inequality and segregation. Meetings of the organization were often disrupted by white mobs, while individual members of the NAACP were threatened, harassed, and occasionally murdered. Despite these acts of violence, the NAACP moved forward with its agenda for achieving civil rights for African Americans.

One of the NAACP's strongest weapons in its fight to end discrimination was its publication, *The Crisis*. DuBois was chosen to manage the publication, and the first issue was published in November 1910. The function of *The Crisis* was to update African Americans on the fight for equality. Through his scathing editorials, DuBois reported atrocities and lynchings and offered his opinions on the political and educational problems that African Americans faced.

The NAACP also had a positive effect on African American life by initiating specific challenges to the Jim Crow laws. Through its Legal Redress Committee, the organization focused on barriers to voting, housing segregation, and other forms of discrimination. The legal team adopted a strategy of mounting limited challenges to discrimination at the local level, carefully choosing only those cases that had a likelihood of success. For example, the NAACP lawyers attacked housing segregation at a local level in Louisville, Kentucky, and were successful in having the laws there overturned. Using similar tactics, the NAACP got the grandfather clause declared null and void in several Southern counties. Also, in a number of cities NAACP lawyers got new trials ordered for African Americans who had been convicted of murder. While these cases had little impact on the everyday lives of millions of African Americans living in the South, they laid the foundation for broader legal challenges to Jim Crow.

African American Protest

The NAACP's efforts went well beyond mounting legal challenges, however. For one thing, whereas Booker T. Washington had opposed directly confronting white racism, the NAACP urged its members to protest and agitate for change on a wide front. In the first half of the twentieth century, according to historian Ronald L.F. Davis, "African Americans turned to publicity, legal challenges, bearing witness, self-help and advocacy groups, music, literature, and religion as the cornerstones of their battle against Jim Crow. These expressions of resistance flowed into a river of protest that engulfed the nation."[67]

African American poet Claude McKay in his poem *If We Must Die* wrote of this new black resistance, exhorting his readers to fight, even if it meant dying.

As the anger expressed in McKay's poem suggests, a new generation of African Americans, born into freedom, not slavery, was growing increasingly resentful of white repression. At the same time, within every black community there were leaders—businessmen, ministers, and educators—who were willing to work with white politicians and who used their powers of persuasion to obtain certain kinds of assistance. This was especially true in Southern cities that were home to large black populations. In these communities at least a few individuals had managed to beat the odds and register to vote. Needing the support of even this small number of voters, white politicians agreed to provide assistance in exchange for African American support. This intervention might take the form of asking a judge to reduce the length of jail sentences or getting money for a black school. Black leaders also had the ability to call boycotts of white-owned businesses that served their communities; white merchants would, therefore, ask politicians to do favors for the black community, knowing it was in their interests to do so.

The Harlem Renaissance

At the same time that blacks who had stayed in the South were finally beginning to chop away at the walls thrown up by white racism, a few of those who had left the South during the first two decades of the twentieth century were mounting a different sort of assault on bigotry. Hoping to find work and better living conditions in the North, tens of thousands of blacks had made their way to New York City where they found housing in a section of the city called Harlem.

In 1917 members of the NAACP march in protest of lynching laws. The NAACP urged members across the United States to agitate for social change.

Langston Hughes

There were many great African American voices that contributed to the Harlem Renaissance. One of the most prolific of those voices was that of James Langston Hughes. Hughes, from an early age, was interested in expressing himself through poetry and other forms of literature. He wrote his first poem at the age of eight and was designated "Class Poet" by his elementary school classmates. Despite being encouraged by his father to pursue a more profitable career, Hughes persisted in his literary efforts.

Settling in Harlem, New York, in the early 1920s, Hughes devoted his entire life to writing about the hardships of African American life during the Jim Crow years. Highly critical of African Americans who accepted segregation, he encouraged black authors to find their own unique voices and to speak out about the realities of black life. In his own work Hughes exhorted blacks to take pride in their color and their heritage.

Perhaps his most memorable character was a man named Jesse B. Semple. In a series of books and essays, Hughes spoke through Semple and offered his opinion about a wide variety of subjects. He used his character to speak out against segregation, while also offering a positive viewpoint of what a black man could achieve if he had the drive and the determination to succeed.

His poems, short plays, essays, and short stories appeared in many publications, including the NAACP publication *The Crisis*. Widely read throughout the United States, Hughes was ultimately inducted into the National Institute of Arts and Letters in 1961, following a career that spanned five decades.

Writer Langston Hughes was the most prolific voice of the Harlem Renaissance.

Harlem was also where black leaders such as DuBois chose to settle. As a result, by 1920 Harlem had become the intellectual and social capital of black America. DuBois believed that black writers and poets could produce works that would be politically powerful, and he encouraged the creation of such works by publishing them in the NAACP's journal *The Crisis*. The intellectual ferment created by this potent mix of politics and art resulted in an explosion of literary, musical, and artistic creativity known as the Harlem Renaissance. What united participants in this endeavor was their sense of taking part in a common cause and their commitment to giving artistic expression to the African American experience. The Harlem Renaissance was, therefore, characterized by a strong sense of racial pride and a desire for social and political equality.

As DuBois and his fellow activists had hoped, black artists used art and their growing celebrity to challenge Jim Crow at every opportunity. In doing so, they helped raise the nation's awareness of the hardships faced by African Americans. Achievements were made in nearly all fields of creative and artistic endeavor. Jazz and blues, for example, saw the emergence of such notable musicians as Louis Armstrong, Bessie Smith, and Billie Holiday. Holiday, in one of her masterpieces, *Strange Fruit,* evoked the horrors of lynching by comparing the hanging bodies of victims to fruit.

The talent of these and other African American musicians caught the attention of well-to-do whites, who streamed into nightclubs such as Harlem's Cotton Club to hear black entertainers perform.

Literature and poetry alike spoke of blacks overcoming a sorrowful and violent past. During the 1920s over fifty works of African American poetry and fiction were published. Historian C. Vann Woodward elaborates: "New poets and novelists gained national attention by giving voice to the ancient wrongs, the brooding sorrows, and the mounting indignation of their race."[68]

The Harlem Renaissance, however, while vital to the development of African Americans artists, did little to touch the lives of the majority of black Americans who remained mired in poverty. Even the nightclubs where the musical stars performed practiced strict segregation; the only blacks who heard the performances

Idlewild: An African American Resort

███

During the early twentieth century the shores of Lake Michigan were a favorite summer destination for thousands of white vacationers. Segregation, however, prevented African Americans from renting or owning homes in the area or staying in resorts. Black middle-class families from Midwestern cities, seeking a vacation spot of their own, eventually began congregating in the small black town of Idlewild, located some thirty miles east in Michigan's Lake County. The concept of a black resort was welcome to those who had encountered discrimination in their previous vacation travels.

Idlewild increased in popularity during the 1920s and 1930s when the area's residents and entrepreneurs decided to promote the town as a place to attend performances by some of the leading black entertainers of the time. Idlewild Clubhouse was built on a small island in Idlewild Lake as a venue to accommodate singers and performers that would include Sarah Vaughn, Louis Armstrong, B.B. King, Aretha Franklin, and Sammy Davis Jr.

The resort's growth continued through the 1950s. Hotels and restaurants were opened along with riding stables, recreation centers, public beaches, nightclubs, and taverns. Hundreds of homes and rental cottages were built to accommodate African American vacationers, who often numbered over twenty thousand a day. With the coming of integration in the 1960s, however, Idlewild's popularity diminished as African American vacationers were able to stay in previously all-white lodgings and locales.

were the waiters and other staff who served the well-heeled white patrons.

Eventually, the Harlem Renaissance ended as the Great Depression of the 1930s resulted in the flood of wealthy visitors to Harlem being reduced to a trickle and then drying up altogether. Despite the end of this cultural explosion, African Americans had found hope in the works of the movement's artists. This hope would translate into a new appreciation for the potential their own race held and a determination to fight for change throughout America in the decades ahead.

Chapter Six

The Beginning of the End for Jim Crow

The decades of the 1940s and 1950s saw the beginning of the end for the Jim Crow system in the United States, but it was not an easy beginning, nor was it an easy end. In fact, the federal government's response to the Great Depression, in the form of programs aimed at improving the economy, often were structured in such a way as to exclude African Americans from participating or benefiting from them.

World War II likewise brought immense challenges to the United States, yet the nation often resisted taking advantage of the potential contributions of its black citizens. In the South, the Jim Crow system was so ingrained that it even resisted the intervention of the federal government. Not until a handful of courageous African American lawyers stubbornly brought case after case before the federal courts did real change begin to occur.

Roosevelt Ends Federal Segregation

African Americans had reason to hope for an improvement in their lives when Franklin D. Roosevelt became president in 1932. At that time the United States was in the midst of a severe depression that left the economy at its lowest point in American history. Among the hardest hit by the depression were millions of African Americans who found themselves in even deeper poverty. Promising jobs for all Americans and an end to poverty, Roosevelt set forth a wide-sweeping program of reforms called the New Deal.

However, Roosevelt was a pragmatist who was willing to make deals with anyone, including segregationists, in order to get the votes he needed in Congress to implement his reforms. As a result, and despite the input of several African American advisers, the New Deal reforms that blacks hoped for failed to materialize. The Social Security Act of 1935, for instance, provided unemployment benefits to millions of Americans. Yet, since the law excluded domestic work-

In 1935 President Franklin Delano Roosevelt signs one of his New Deal reforms. Unfortunately, Roosevelt's New Deal failed to improve the lot of most blacks.

ers and agricultural laborers, the majority of African American workers were ineligible for benefits. By 1940 many African Americans were often heard referring to the New Deal as the Dirty Deal.

Even the outbreak of war and the increased demand for labor in newly created munitions and other defense-related industries failed to benefit many black workers. African Americans, like other Americans, eagerly applied for jobs in the defense industry. But while thousands of whites were hired, most blacks were turned away. For example, the Southern Welding Institute had trained and qualified nearly two hundred African Americans as arc welders, a class of worker urgently needed in shipyards. None of these graduates, however, were able to find jobs in Southern plants and shipyards despite being qualified. Kansas City Standard Steel's response to black workers epitomized the attitude of many white employers: "We have not had a Negro worker in twenty-five years and do not plan to start now."[69]

African American leaders sought the help of the federal government in ending discriminatory hiring in defense plants. Under the leadership of African American labor organizer A. Philip Randolph, a massive protest march was planned for January 1941 in the nation's capital. Randolph, in speaking to his followers, reiterated the reason for the march: "Let us march ten thousand strong on Washington, D.C. to demand the right to work and fight for our country."[70] The prospect of thousands of protesters in the streets alarmed Roosevelt, who feared the damage such a march would inflict on his image as someone concerned about the downtrodden. The president, therefore, met with Randolph and agreed to meet some of his demands.

On June 25, 1941, Roosevelt issued Executive Order 8802, which "prohibited discrimination on the basis of race, creed, or color in certain areas of federal employment, vocational training programs administered by federal agencies, and the national defense industry."[71] Roosevelt also established the Fair Employment Practices Committee for the purpose of investigating charges of discrimination in these agencies and businesses.

Public Opinion

Roosevelt's order resulted in greater hiring of blacks in America's defense industry, but it was not until the mid- to late 1940s that a changing

In the 1940s, Swedish economist Gunnar Myrdal studied the status of African Americans in the South.

attitude on the part of the American public became apparent. This change in part resulted from groundbreaking work by Gunnar Myrdal, a Swedish economist who had been hired by the Carnegie Corporation to study the status of African Americans in the United States. Over a period of several years Myrdal traveled through the South, interviewing African Americans about their lives and problems. Based on his research, in 1944 Myrdal published a fifteen-hundred-page, two-volume work titled *An American Dilemma: The Negro Problem and Modern Democracy.*

Myrdal's conclusion that white bigotry kept African Americans in an inferior position was in marked contrast to the prevailing belief that blacks were inherently inferior. Using graphic depictions of the conditions that African Americans faced in the South, along with documented evidence of the violence perpetrated against blacks, Myrdal presented a horrifying picture of the Jim Crow system. Readers found Myrdal's apparent objectivity persuasive. Although the book was condemned in the South, it was widely read in the North, especially by well-educated whites who found Myrdal's conclusions thought-provoking and alarming.

Another voice challenging segregation was Frank Boas, a well-known American sociologist and anthropologist. He funded an in-depth study of African Americans and concluded: "The so-called Negro Problem was not blacks' innate inferiority and inability to fit into American society as was commonly believed, but rather an American environment that had shaped and continued to oppress them."[72] In light of the conclusions of these two authors, to much of the American public the Jim Crow system became a national embarrassment.

Adding to the growing public outrage about Jim Crow was the fight against German dictator Adolf Hitler. Hitler espoused the concept of the Master Race and the elimination of "lesser" races. The American public was finding it more and more difficult to condone discrimination and the lack of equality at home while it supported fighting to free Europe from the Nazis.

The End of Segregation in the Military

Despite the end of segregation in federal programs and defense industries and changing public opinion regarding race, Roosevelt had done little to end discrimination against African Americans in the military. Needing the support of Southern congressmen and Southern industrialists, Roosevelt was unwilling to speak out against segregation in the armed services. The failure to address this discrimination drew the ire of African American soldiers and their families. The wife of a black soldier spoke for many when she wrote: "We're fighting a war now to insure freedom of opportunity to everybody. . . . If the American Negro is not going to enjoy equally in the fruits of democracy, why then should our men in the armed services be maimed or die on foreign soil . . . when here in the South their lives are made a virtual hell on earth?"[73]

An end to segregation in the military only came more than two years after Roosevelt's death in office. Under pressure from the NAACP, his successor, Harry S. Truman, issued Executive Order 9981 on July 26, 1948. This new law required "equality of treatment and opportunity for all persons in the armed services without regard to race, color, religion, or national origin."[74]

Truman and Civil Rights

Despite this executive order, segregation remained a reality for African American veterans when they returned home after World War II. As had happened after World War I, returning black soldiers were met with hostility and violence. A rash of postwar lynchings committed against black veterans so appalled Truman that he decided to bring the issue of civil rights into full public view. In 1946 he appointed the first-ever President's Committee on Civil Rights.

The new committee met for several months and in 1947 issued a report titled "To Secure These Rights." Among its recommendations were antilynching laws, laws to prevent racial discrimination at voter registration, and the establishment of a civil rights section within the Justice Department. The committee also advised Truman to end segregation in interstate public transportation and to block federal money from going to companies that practiced segregation.

Truman took the recommendations seriously and incorporated most of the suggestions into the first civil rights legislation introduced to Congress in over eighty years. "Many of our people still suffer the indignity of insult, the narrowing fear of intimidation, and, I regret to say, the threat of physical and mob violence," Truman asserted. "We cannot wait another decade or another generation to remedy these evils. We must work as never before, to cure them now."[75] Despite the lofty goals Truman's words pronounced, the president was realistic enough to know that his civil rights package stood little chance of passage due to the presence of powerful Southerners in Congress.

Truman's support of civil rights, in fact, led many members of the Democratic Party to form their own splinter group, known as the Dixiecrat or States' Rights Party. Supporting South Carolina senator Strom Thurmond for president, an outspoken advocate of segregation, the Dixiecrats received over 1 million popular votes in the election of 1948. After a very narrow presidential victory in 1948, Truman abandoned many of his earlier stances in an attempt to reunify the Democratic Party.

The failure of the Truman administration to pursue its original civil rights agenda frustrated and angered many African Americans. A new generation of black leaders moved to the forefront, showing a readiness to fight against segregation and discrimination. And yet, for the moment, they made little headway in effecting any positive changes. "Blacks remained invisible as individuals to most whites and inferior as a group," opines historian Goldfield. "Shut away in 'nigger towns,' segregated in public schools, excluded from parks, restaurants, clubs, and most occupations . . . blacks for the most part remained in their designated place."[76]

The Legal Counsel of the NAACP

Knowing that little was changing in African American communities, the NAACP and its legal counsel returned to the strategy of challenging the Jim Crow laws in the courts. From the beginning,

Thurgood Marshall

Thurgood Marshall, born in 1908, grew up in the South and experienced racism and discrimination firsthand. He enrolled at Lincoln University in Chester, Pennsylvania, and soon took part in his first civil rights protest. He and twenty-five friends refused to sit in the black section of a local theater. Rather than pressing charges, the theater changed its seating arrangement. This action was the first of many that Marshall took against the Jim Crow laws and practices that prohibited African Americans from living a life of equality.

Attending Howard University School of Law in Washington D.C., Marshall was hand-picked by Charles Hamilton Houston to join the NAACP Legal Defense Fund. Nicknamed "Mr. Civil Rights," Marshall worked tirelessly to end segregation. He dedicated his entire legal career to striking down unjust laws and winning social equality for African Americans. His most famous case, *Brown v. Board of Education of Topeka, Kansas,* heralded the end of school segregation in the South and the beginning of the civil rights movement of the 1950s and 1960s.

After six decades of legal work, during which he argued and won more cases before the Supreme Court than any other American, Marshall was himself appointed to the Court in 1967 by President Lyndon Baines Johnson, becoming the first African American to serve on the highest court in the land. His record on the Court was exemplary; he defended the rights of immigrants, supported the right of privacy, and established a record for defending the rights of minority groups. He retired from the Court in 1991, and died in 1993.

In 1967 Thurgood Marshall (standing) became the first African American appointed to the Supreme Court.

As head of the NAACP's legal team, Charles Hamilton Houston challenged Jim Crow laws that prohibited blacks from attending white colleges.

the NAACP had imposed two criteria for their acceptance of a legal case. First of all the case had to involve discrimination and injustice; more importantly, it had to establish some kind of legal precedent or serve as an example for similar cases in the future. In other words, the issue had to involve the protection or attainment of some civil rights for African Americans as a group.

Heading the legal team for the NAACP was Charles Hamilton Houston, who in 1934 was appointed special legal counsel to that organization. Houston was born in 1895, the year before the Supreme Court's ruling in *Plessy v. Ferguson* had given "separate but equal" official sanction. After graduating from Harvard Law School, Houston had devoted his legal career to overturning *Plessy v. Ferguson*. Houston proposed to attack Jim Crow at what he considered its most vulnerable point—education. "Here," he later recalled, "racial discrimination was clear, gross, and easy to document."[77] It was easy, Houston asserted, to photograph dilapidated African American schools and compare the pictures with photos of new schools reserved for whites.

Using his position as dean of the Howard University School of Law, Houston recruited bright and ambitious African American lawyers to join the NAACP legal team. Together with his most adept student, Thurgood Marshall, Houston traveled throughout the South looking for cases of school segregation that could be brought before the federal court system.

Challenging Jim Crow on the University Level

Houston and Marshall during the 1930s and 1940s had focused their initial efforts on higher education and those African Americans who were trying to gain admittance to white universities. They chose this avenue primarily because the "separate but equal" fiction was glaringly difficult to maintain at the college level. After winning *Murray v. Maryland,* in which the University of Maryland was ordered by the Supreme Court in 1936 to admit African American Donald G. Murray to law school, the two lawyers turned their attention to a case in Missouri.

The University of Missouri had refused to admit African American Lloyd Lionel Gaines to its law school in 1938, suggesting he attend school somewhere else or wait until a separate facility for African Americans could be built. Houston took the case to the Supreme Court, where in *Missouri v. Canada* (Canada was the name of the university registrar who had denied Gaines admittance to the school) the Court ruled that the states had a clear obligation to provide equal education for all their citizens. The justices further ruled that a state could not expect an African American student to wait while a separate school building was built.

Another significant ruling took place in 1948. In that year a federal district court ordered the University of Oklahoma to admit George McLaurin, an African American doctoral student in education. Goldfield describes the university's actions following this ruling:

The university administrator, determined to enforce segregation in some form, and perhaps hoping to discourage McLaurin and other blacks from challenging the system again, forced McLaurin to sit at a desk in an anteroom outside his classroom, provided a segregated desk in a dingy corner of the library, and allowed him to use the cafeteria only at odd hours, and to eat only at a specific table. [78]

Houston and his team took the case to the Supreme Court, where the justices ruled that such restrictions were unconstitutional. Even before the ruling was handed down, however, many white graduate students had shown their displeasure with the university's policy by sitting and eating with McLaurin.

Elementary Education

While these cases did not completely end segregation at the university level, the victories bolstered the NAACP's determination to keep fighting. The NAACP and its legal counsel turned to public education on the elementary level as their next focus of attack. In the late 1940s and early 1950s the NAACP began to gather cases from several states, involving young African American students who had been denied admission to white public schools.

At that time there were over 2 million African American children in segregated elementary schools throughout the South. There was no question that the quality of education these youngsters received was far inferior to what their white peers were receiving. Litwack elaborates: "No matter how it was measured—by the quality of the facilities, the length of the school term, financial appropriations, student-teacher ratio, curriculum, teacher's preparation, and salaries—the education available to black children in the . . . South was vastly inferior to that available to white children." [79]

The NAACP, however, knew that it would not be enough to simply document the inferiority of black schools; the detrimental effects of that inferiority would have to be proven. Historian Sanford Wexler explains: "In order to establish the fact that separate schools could never be truly equal, the NAACP Legal Defense Fund had to prove that the consequence of segregation, including psychological, intellectual, and financial damages, prevented genuine equality from taking place." [80]

To support this position the NAACP turned to psychologist Kenneth Clark, who tested hundreds of black school children between the ages of six and nine. "These children," Clark later testified, "saw themselves as inferior and they accepted the inferiority as part of reality." [81] Other sociologists and psychologists supported Clark's findings and further reported that children who felt inferior always performed poorly academically.

Doctoral student George McLaurin sits outside an all-white classroom at the University of Oklahoma. In 1948 the Supreme Court ruled that the university's segregation policy was unconstitutional.

Brown v. Board of Education

In the early 1950s the NAACP's legal counsel found the case they were looking for. In Topeka, Kansas, eleven-year-old Linda Brown and twelve other black students had been denied permission to attend a white school. Represented by Thurgood Marshall, who had taken Houston's place as chief legal counsel for the NAACP, the families sued the Topeka Board of Education, claiming that segregated schools were a violation of the Fourteenth Amendment. The cases were listed alphabetically; Linda Brown's name came first and *Brown v. Board of Education of Topeka, Kansas,* went to district court in Kansas.

Kansas judge Walter Huxman ruled in favor of Brown and the other children, agreeing with the psychologists that Marshall had used as witnesses. He issued the following statement:

> Segregation of white and colored children in public schools has a detrimental effect upon colored children. The impact is greater when it has the sanction of the law; for the policy of separating the races is usually interpreted as denoting the inferiority of the Negro group. A sense of inferiority affects the motivation of a child to learn.[82]

Huxman's decision, however, was later overturned in a higher court, at which time Marshall and his group of lawyers decided to appeal the case to the U.S. Supreme Court, which first heard arguments for the case in 1952. The justices deliberated for eighteen months and even asked to hear a second round of arguments before making a ruling. Shortly before noon on Monday, May 17, 1954, they announced their decision. Chief Justice Earl Warren read the unanimous decision of the Court. The heart of the decision was contained in two sentences: "We conclude, unanimously, that in the field of public education, the doctrine of separate but equal has no place. Separate educational facilities are inherently unequal."[83]

African Americans throughout the United States felt energized and empowered by this decision. White reaction to the ruling in the South, however, was swift and unrepentant. Senator James O. East-

Linda Brown (front row, third from left) sits with other plaintiffs in the landmark 1954 *Brown v. Board of Education* school segregation case.

The End of Segregation in Baseball

Like the rest of American life during the Jim Crow era, all sporting events were strictly segregated. Thousands of talented African American athletes were denied access to major league sports and forced to play in various Negro leagues. Segregation in sports, however, came to an end in the late 1940s when Jackie Robinson was hired by the Brooklyn Dodgers of New York.

Born on January 31, 1919, in a sharecropper's farmhouse in Georgia, Robinson went on to attend UCLA in California and lettered in four different sports. After serving in the U.S. Army, Robinson signed up to play baseball for the Negro National League. Meanwhile, Brooklyn Dodgers owner and manager Branch Rickey was one baseball executive who had decided that racism had no place in sports. He was on the lookout for an African American player to break the racial barrier in baseball and signed Robinson to a contract with the Dodgers in 1947.

Many whites and all African Americans applauded the move and said it was long overdue. A large number of whites, including many white ballplayers, however, objected. Many opposing players deliberately threw pitches at Robinson's head and spiked him with their cleats on the basepaths. Fans shouted "nigger" at him when he came to bat and often threw stones at him. When the team traveled, Robinson was forced to stay in rundown hotels reserved for blacks and to eat alone, because Jim Crow laws dictated that blacks could not eat or stay in the same establishments as whites. Robinson also received hundreds of death threats and thousands of pieces of hate mail. Despite these conditions, Robinson went on to become not only Rookie of the Year in 1947 but a member of the Baseball Hall of Fame.

land of Mississippi condemned the actions of the Court and spoke for many whites: "The South will not abide by nor obey this legislative decision by a political court."[84] Calling the day the Court handed down its ruling Black Monday, Eastland urged Southern states to ignore the decision and continue their segregation policies.

Despite the reaction of white Southerners, the decision of the Supreme Court heralded the beginning of the end for the Jim Crow era. Most historians agree that this case was the most important legal issue decided by the Supreme Court in the twentieth century. Wexler elaborates: "The *Brown* decision marked the turning point in which the nation was finally willing to face the consequences of centuries of racial discrimination."[85]

Brown II

The Supreme Court decision, however, did not put an immediate end to the Jim Crow system, since the Court did not set a deadline for the end of segregated schools. The justices heard further arguments during the next twelve months to determine the best way to integrate the nation. In 1955, in a second case commonly known as *Brown II* the Court issued a ruling that called for "all deliberate speed" in dismantling segregation throughout the country. That summer the NAACP filed petitions for desegregation with over 170 school boards in the South.

While the Court had called for all deliberate speed, the reality was that the process of desegregation was extremely slow. Whites throughout the country only reluctantly accepted integration. African American scholar Roger Wilkins suggests that this reluctance was based on the idea that privilege and racial identity could not be separated:

> It turned out that intensively in the South—and to a surprisingly large degree in the North as well—the privileges, both material and psychic, that accrued to whites from racism had grown into the lives of the people. . . . Whiteness and its advantages had become emotionally and deeply valued parts of the identities of many whites. . . . Men in white shirts and suits in Congress and in executive suites all over the South devised plans to undermine the *Brown* decision. They were all engaged in an emotional defense of who they deemed themselves to be and of what they knew they were entitled to have.[86]

White supremacy and racism was so ingrained into American society that it would take continuous pressure from African American leaders and a massive protest movement to achieve the end of separate but equal facilities in the South and elsewhere. Jim Crow, however, was doomed and African Americans were poised to at last take their place as full participants in American society.

Notes

Introduction: A Dream Deferred

1. Roy L. Brooks, *Rethinking the American Race Problem.* Berkeley: University of California Press, 1990, p. 3.
2. David M. Kennedy, *Freedom from Fear.* New York: Oxford University Press, 1999, p. 764.
3. Quoted in David Halberstam, ed., *Defining a Nation.* Washington, DC: National Geographic Books, 2003, p. 83.

Chapter One: Maintaining White Supremacy

4. Quoted in Sanford Wexler, *The Civil Rights Movement.* New York: Facts On File, 1993, p. 18.
5. Philip Dray, *At the Hands of Persons Unknown: The Lynching of Black America.* New York: Random House, 2002, p. 35.
6. Robert E. Martin, "Jump Jim Crow," *Encyclopedia Americana Online.* http://sunsite3.berkeley.edu/calheritage/Jimcrow/glossary.html.
7. John Hope Franklin and Alfred A. Moss Jr., *From Slavery to Freedom,* 8th ed. New York: Alfred A. Knopf, 2004, p. 259.
8. David R. Goldfield, *Black, White, and Southern.* Baton Rouge: Louisiana State University Press, 1990, p. 74.
9. Quoted in Leon F. Litwack, *Trouble in Mind: Black Southerners in the Age of Jim Crow.* New York: Alfred A. Knopf, 1998, p. 228.
10. Quoted in Litwack, *Trouble in Mind,* p. 226.

Chapter Two: Separate but Equal: The Jim Crow System

11. Goldfield, *Black, White, and Southern,* p. 13.
12. Adam Fairclough, *Better Day Coming: Blacks and Equality, 1890–2000.* New York: Viking, 2001, p. 13.
13. Quoted in Dray, *At the Hands of Persons Unknown,* p. 97.
14. Quoted in Litwack, *Trouble in Mind,* p. 181.
15. Quoted in Litwack, *Trouble in Mind,* p. 205.
16. Quoted in Halberstam, *Defining a Nation,* p. 74.
17. Quoted in Grace Elizabeth Hale, *Making Whiteness: The Culture of Segregation in the South, 1890–1940.* New York: Vintage, 1998, p. 131.
18. Quoted in Dray, *At the Hands of Persons Unknown,* p. 57.
19. Quoted in Litwack, *Trouble in Mind,* p. 335.
20. Quoted in Litwack, *Trouble in Mind,* p. 95.
21. Franklin and Moss, *From Slavery to Freedom,* p. 445.
22. Quoted in Halberstam, *Defining a Nation,* p. 75.

23. Franklin and Moss, *From Slavery to Freedom,* p. 343.

24. Quoted in Wexler, *The Civil Rights Movement,* p. 22.

25. Quoted in Dray, *At the Hands of Persons Unknown,* p. 111.

26. Quoted in Wexler, *The Civil Rights Movement,* p. 6.

27. Quoted in Wexler, *The Civil Rights Movement,* p. 25.

28. Franklin and Moss, *From Slavery to Freedom,* p. 291.

Chapter Three: Life Under Jim Crow

29. Quoted in C. Vann Woodward, *The Strange Career of Jim Crow.* New York: Oxford University Press, 1966, p. 96.

30. Quoted in Wexler, *The Civil Rights Movement,* p. 2.

31. Quoted in Stephen Ambrose and Douglas Brinkley, *Witness to America.* New York: HarperCollins, 1999, p. 393.

32. Litwack, *Trouble in Mind,* p. 169.

33. Goldfield, *Black, White, and Southern,* p. 25.

34. Quoted in Hale, *Making Whiteness,* p. 136.

35. Litwack, *Trouble in Mind,* p. 10.

36. Quoted in Litwack, *Trouble in Mind,* p. 217.

37. Fairclough, *Better Day Coming,* p. 162.

38. Litwack, *Trouble in Mind,* p. 391.

39. Quoted in Franklin and Moss, *From Slavery to Freedom,* p. 349.

Chapter Four: Violence and Injustice

40. Dray, *At the Hands of Persons Unknown,* p. xi.

41. Quoted in Litwack, *Trouble in Mind,* p. 57.

42. Mark Gado, "The History of Lynching," in *Lynching in America: Carnival of Death,* Court TV's Crime Library, Courtroom Television Network LLC. http://crimelibrary.com/notorious_murders/mass/lynching/lynching_2.html.

43. Litwack, *Trouble in Mind,* p. 308.

44. Quoted in Litwack, *Trouble in Mind,* p. 309.

45. Litwack, *Trouble in Mind,* p. 285.

46. Hale, *Making Whiteness,* p. 201.

47. Dray, *At the Hands of Persons Unknown,* p. 81.

48. Franklin and Moss, *From Slavery to Freedom,* p. 388.

49. Quoted in Richard A. Wormser, "Jim Crow Stories: Events: Red Summer," *The Rise and Fall of Jim Crow,* PBS. www.pbs.org/wnet/jimcrow/stories_events/red.html.

50. Robert A. Gibson, "The Negro Holocaust: Lynching and Race Riots in the United States," Yale-New Haven Teachers Institute. www.yale.edu/ynhti/curriculum/units/1979/2/79.02.04.x.html.

51. Quoted in Gibson, "The Negro Holocaust."

52. Litwack, *Trouble in Mind,* p. 264.

53. Litwack, *Trouble in Mind,* p. 248.

54. Quoted in Dray, *At the Hands of Persons Unknown,* p. 281.

55. Litwack, *Trouble in Mind,* p. 427.

56. Quoted in Linda O. McMurry, *To Keep the Waters Troubled: The Life of Ida B. Wells.* New York: Oxford University Press, 1998, p. 136.

57. Quoted in McMurry, *To Keep the Waters Troubled,* p. 228.

Chapter Five: Accommodation or Protest: Responding to Jim Crow

58. Quoted in William S. McFeely, *Frederick Douglass.* New York: W.W. Norton, 1991, p. 139.
59. Fairclough, *Better Day Coming,* p. 44.
60. Booker T. Washington, *Up from Slavery.* New York: Penguin, 1986, p. 281.
61. Dray, *At the Hands of Persons Unknown,* p. 116.
62. Quoted in Benjamin Quarles, *The Negro in the Making of America.* New York: Touchstone, 1996, p. 203.
63. Fairclough, *Better Days Coming,* p. 54.
64. Franklin and Moss, *From Slavery to Freedom,* p. 351.
65. Quoted in Franklin and Moss, *From Slavery to Freedom,* p. 352.
66. Quoted in Wexler, *The Civil Rights Movement,* p. 9.
67. Ronald L.F. Davis, "Resisting Jim Crow," *History of Jim Crow.* www.jimcrowhistory.org/history/resisting2.htm.
68. Woodward, *The Strange Career of Jim Crow,* p. 125.

Chapter Six: The Beginning of the End for Jim Crow

69. Quoted in Kennedy, *Freedom from Fear,* p. 765.
70. Quoted in Fairclough, *Better Day Coming,* p. 155.
71. Quoted in Brooks, *Rethinking the American Race Problem,* p. 26.
72. Quoted in Dray, *At the Hands of Persons Unknown,* p. 298.
73. Quoted in Fairclough, *Better Day Coming,* p. 192.
74. Quoted in Brooks, *Rethinking the American Race Problem,* p. 27.
75. Quoted in Dray, *At the Hands of Persons Unknown,* p. 384.
76. Goldfield, *Black, White, and Southern,* p. 75.
77. Quoted in Fairclough, *Better Day Coming,* p. 198.
78. Goldfield, *Black, White, and Southern,* p. 59.
79. Litwack, *Trouble in Mind,* p. 107.
80. Wexler, *The Civil Rights Movement,* p. 32.
81. Quoted in Wexler, *The Civil Rights Movement,* p. 34.
82. Quoted in Halberstam, *Defining a Nation,* p. 80.
83. Quoted in Woodward, *The Strange Career of Jim Crow,* p. 147.
84. Quoted in Wexler, *The Civil Rights Movement,* p. 39.
85. Wexler, *The Civil Rights Movement,* p. 39.
86. Quoted in Halberstam, *Defining a Nation,* p. 82.

For Further Reading

Books

Maury Allen, *Jackie Robinson: A Life Remembered.* New York: Franklin Watts, 1987. A biography of the great baseball player who was the first African American to play in the major leagues.

Reggie Finlayson, *We Shall Overcome.* Minneapolis: Lerner, 2003. While primarily concerned with the era of the civil rights movement, there is some material about the Jim Crow era.

Maria Fleming, *A Place at the Table: Struggle for Equality in America.* New York: Oxford University Press, 2001. This book deals with many issues and includes a good chapter on racial equality.

Dennis Brindell Fradin and Judith Bloom Fradin, *Ida B. Wells: Mother of the Civil Rights Movement.* New York: Clarion, 2000. A biography of Ida B. Wells, well-known African American writer whose efforts to publicize lynching influenced generations of Americans.

Deborah Hitzeroth and Sharon Leon, *The Importance of Thurgood Marshall.* San Diego: Lucent, 1997. An excellent biography about this important African American lawyer and Supreme Court justice.

Stuart Kallen, *The Civil Rights Movement.* Minneapolis: Rockbottom, 1990. This book has a good section on the Jim

Crow era as it affected the later civil rights movement.

Patricia C. McKissack, *Mary McLeod Bethune: A Great American Educator.* Chicago: Childrens, 1985. An excellent biography of this African American woman who was instrumental in establishing schools for African Americans.

Patricia C. McKissack and Frederick McKissack, *W.E.B. DuBois.* New York: Franklin Watts, 1990. An excellent biography of this African American leader and writer.

Zak Mettger, *Reconstruction: America After the Civil War.* New York: Lodestar, 1994. This is an excellent book about the post–Civil War period and events leading up to the Jim Crow era.

Milton Mettzer, *There Comes a Time: The Struggle for Civil Rights.* New York: Random House, 2001. A book about the long struggle for African American freedom and equality.

Walter Dean Myers, *Now Is Your Time: The African American Struggle for Freedom.* New York: HarperCollins, 1991. This book traces African American history from colonial times through the latter part of the twentieth century. There is a good section on the Jim Crow era.

Gerald Newman and Eleanor Newman Layfield, *Racism: Divided by Color.* Springfield, NJ: Enslow, 1995. This book gives an excellent overview of racism and the problems it causes.

Andrea Davis Pickney, *Let It Shine: Stories of Black Women Freedom Fighters.* San Diego: Gulliver, 2000. This book includes biographical sketches of important African American women and their roles in fighting segregation.

Darren Rhym, *The NAACP.* Philadelphia: Chelsea House, 2002. An excellent book about the history of the National Association for the Advancement of Colored People.

Sharman Apt Russell, *Frederick Douglass.* New York: Chelsea House, 1988. A biography of this African American abolitionist and promoter on behalf of racial equality.

Howard Smead, *The Afro-Americans.* New York: Chelsea House, 1989. This excellent book looks at African American history from its origins in Africa to the late 1980s. There is a good section on the Jim Crow era.

Reginald Wilson, *Think About Our Rights: Civil Liberties in the United States.* New York: Walker, 1988. This book focuses on all aspects of civil rights and includes a good section on the Jim Crow laws.

Web Sites

Guide to Black History (http://search.eb. com/blackhistory/micro/179/2.html). This *Encylopedia Britannica* site presents a wide variety of articles and film clips about people, places, and events in black history.

Jim Crow America (www.ushmm.org/ museum/exhibit/online/olympics/zcc0 36a.htm). A photographic Web site featuring pictures from the Jim Crow era.

Langston Hughes (www.gale.com/free_ resources/bhm/bio/hughes_1.htm). This site offers the biography of African American poet and author Langston Hughes along with access to the biographies of other well-known African Americans.

Works Consulted

Books

Stephen Ambrose and Douglas Brinkley, *Witness to America*. New York: Harper-Collins, 1999. Two award-winning historians present an overall history of the United States. The book includes good sections on Reconstruction, Jim Crow, and the Ku Klux Klan.

Roy L. Brooks, *Rethinking the American Race Problem*. Berkeley: University of California Press, 1990. This book gives an overall look at the question of race in America with an emphasis on civil rights laws of the past and present.

Gail Buckley, *American Patriots: The Story of Blacks in the Military*. New York: Random House, 2001. This journalist for the *Los Angeles Times* and *New York Times* covers the role of African Americans in the military from the Revolution to Desert Storm. She presents excellent coverage of the effect Jim Crow laws had on African Americans in the military.

Philip Dray, *At the Hands of Persons Unknown: The Lynching of Black America*. New York: Random House, 2002. This is an outstanding book that covers the history of lynchings and the reasons behind these crimes, mainly committed against African Americans.

John Egerton, *Speak Now Against the Day*. New York: Alfred A. Knopf, 1994. This book deals with the twenty-five-year period prior to the beginning of the civil rights movement of the 1950s and 1960s.

Adam Fairclough, *Better Day Coming: Blacks and Equality, 1890–2000*. New York: Viking, 2001. This book examines the years of the Jim Crow era with an emphasis on the growing role of African American leaders and protesters.

Eric Foner, *Reconstruction: America's Unfinished Revolution, 1863–1877*. New York: Harper and Row, 1988. This book presents an excellent look at this period of history and places emphasis on the Black Codes, the forerunner of Jim Crow.

John Hope Franklin and Alfred A. Moss Jr., *From Slavery to Freedom*. 8th ed. New York: Alfred A. Knopf, 2004. Both authors have written many books about African American history. This one details African American history from its origins in Africa to the present.

David R. Goldfield, *Black, White, and Southern*. Baton Rouge: Louisiana State University Press, 1990. This author of numerous African American history books focuses on racial relations in the South from 1940 to the present. There is an excellent section on the Jim Crow era.

David Halberstam, ed., *Defining a Nation*. Washington, DC: National Geographic Books, 2003. This book contains an excellent chapter written by Roger Wilkins on racism and Jim Crow. Wilkins is an African American who grew up during the Jim Crow years.

Grace Elizabeth Hale, *Making Whiteness: The Culture of Segregation in the South,*

1890–1940. New York: Vintage, 1998. The author, a professor of history at the University of Virginia, focuses on racial stereotypes and the identification of blackness with inferiority, especially in the South.

David M. Kennedy, *Freedom from Fear*. New York: Oxford University Press, 1999. This book covers the years of the Great Depression and World War II. There are good references to segregation and the roles that African Americans played during this era from 1933 to 1945.

David Levering Lewis, *W.E.B. DuBois: Biography of a Race*. New York: Henry Holt, 1993. An excellent biography of the African American founder of the Niagara Movement and a staunch and outspoken critic of segregation.

Leon F. Litwack, *Trouble in Mind: Black Southerners in the Age of Jim Crow*. New York: Alfred A. Knopf, 1998. This Pulitzer prize–winning author presents an excellent look at the era of Jim Crow and its effect on African Americans in the South.

William S. McFeely, *Frederick Douglass*. New York: W.W. Norton, 1991. This is a biography of the abolitionist and outspoken African American leader of the nineteenth century.

Linda O. McMurry, *To Keep the Waters Troubled: The Life of Ida B. Wells*. New York: Oxford University Press, 1998. The author, a professor of history, presents a biography of one of the earliest and most outspoken critics of lynching.

Benjamin Quarles, *The Negro in the Making of America*. New York: Touchstone, 1996. Originally published in 1964. This noted historian focuses on the role that African Americans have played in American history and includes good coverage of the Jim Crow laws and lynching.

Carl T. Rowan, *Dream Makers, Dream Breakers: The World of Justice Thurgood Marshall*. Boston: Little, Brown, 1993. This book focuses on the life and times of lawyer and Supreme Court justice Thurgood Marshall and his role in ending Jim Crow.

Booker T. Washington, *Up from Slavery*. New York: Penguin, 1986. Originally published by Doubleday in 1901. An autobiography of this influential African American from his birth into slavery to his career as a teacher and speaker.

Sanford Wexler, *The Civil Rights Movement*. New York: Facts On File, 1993. This book offers a good introduction on the origins of the civil rights movement and includes good information on the Jim Crow era.

C. Vann Woodward, *The Strange Career of Jim Crow*. New York: Oxford University Press, 1966. This work by a renowned historian focuses on racial history and the Jim Crow era. The book is based on a series of lectures the author gave at the University of Virginia in the 1950s.

Periodicals

Edward Chappell, "Valentine Museum's Jim Crow," *Nation,* July 17, 1989.

Richard Epstein, "Caste and Civil Rights Laws," *Michigan Law Review,* August 1, 1994.

Martin C. Evans, "Mixed Memories of Jim Crow," *Newsday,* October 16, 2002.

Knight-Ridder News Service, "Project Personalizes Jim Crow," *News and Record,* November 11, 1998.

Lonnae O'Neal Parker, "Days of Jim Crow," *Washington Post,* February 2, 2002.

Internet Sources

Afro-American Almanac, "The Origin of Jim Crow." www.toptags.com/aama/docs/jcrow.htm.

Ronald L.F. Davis, "Creating Jim Crow," *History of Jim Crow.* www.jimcrowhistory.org/history/creating2.htm.

———, "Escaping Jim Crow," *History of Jim Crow.* www.jimcrowhistory.org/history/escaping.htm.

———, "Resisting Jim Crow," *History of Jim Crow.* www.jimcrowhistory.org/history/resisting2.htm.

———, "Surviving Jim Crow," *History of Jim Crow.* www.jimcrowhistory.org/history/surviving2.htm.

Mark Gado, *Lynching in America: Carnival of Death,* Court TV's Crime Library, Courtroom Television Network LLC. www.crimelibrary.com/classics2/carnival.

Robert A. Gibson, "The Negro Holocaust: Lynching and Race Riots in the United States," Yale-New Haven Teachers Institute. www.yale.edu/ynhti/curriculum/units/1979/2/79.02.04.x.html.

Andrew P. Jackson, "James Langston Hughes," *Red Hot Jazz Archive,* February 20, 2005. www.redhotjazz.com/hughes.html.

Robert E. Martin, "Jump Jim Crow," *Encyclopedia Americana Online.* http://sunsite3.berkeley.edu/calheritage/Jimcrow/glossary.html.

Jenny Nolan, "The Luxury Resort That Discrimination Built," *Detroit News.* http://info.detnews.com/history/story/index.cfm?id=121&category=locations.

Richard M. Perloff, "The Press and Lynchings of African Americans," *Journal of Black Studies,* January 2000. http://academic.csuohio.edu/perloffr/lynching.

Stephen Smith, Kate Ellis, and Sasha Aslanian, *Remembering Jim Crow.* http://americanradioworks.publicradio.org/features/remembering/

Soul of America, "Welcome to Nicodemus, Kansas." www.soulofamerica.com/resorts/nicodemus.html.

Thurgood Marshall College, "Thurgood Marshall, Supreme Court Justice," *Center for History and New Media.* http://chnm.gmu.edu/courses/122/hill/marshall.htm.

Allen W. Trelease, "Ku Klux Klan," *Reader's Companion to American History.* http://college.hmco.com/history/readerscomp/rcah/html/rc_051100_kukluxklan.htm.

Richard A. Wormser, "Jim Crow Stories: Events," *The Rise and Fall of Jim Crow,* PBS. www.pbs.org/wnet/jimcrow/stories_events.html.

———, "Jim Crow Stories: People," *The Rise and Fall of Jim Crow,* PBS. www.pbs.org/wnet/jimcrow/stories_people.html.

Robert L. Zangrando, "Lynching," *Reader's Companion to American History.* http://college.hmco.com/history/readerscomp/rcah/html/ah_055200_lynching.htm.

Index

Picture Credits

About the Author

Anne Wallace Sharp is the author of the adult nonfiction book *Gifts,* a compilation of stories about hospice patients; several children's books, including *Daring Women Pirates;* and nine Lucent books. In addition, she has written numerous magazine articles for both the adult and juvenile markets. A retired registered nurse, Sharp has a degree in history. Her other interests include reading, traveling, and spending time with her two grandchildren, Jacob and Nicole. Sharp lives in Beavercreek, Ohio.

What Happens in Winter?

Weather in Winter

by Jenny Fretland VanVoorst

Bullfrog Books

Ideas for Parents and Teachers

Bullfrog Books let children practice reading informational text at the earliest reading levels. Repetition, familiar words, and photo labels support early readers.

Before Reading

- Discuss the cover photo. What does it tell them?
- Look at the picture glossary together. Read and discuss the words.

Read the Book

- "Walk" through the book and look at the photos. Let the child ask questions. Point out the photo labels.
- Read the book to the child, or have him or her read independently.

After Reading

- Prompt the child to think more. Ask: What is winter weather like where you live? What sorts of things do you like to do outside in the winter?

Bullfrog Books are published by Jump!
5357 Penn Avenue South
Minneapolis, MN 55419
www.jumplibrary.com

Library of Congress Cataloging-in-Publication Data

Names: Fretland VanVoorst, Jenny, 1972– author.
Title: Weather in winter / by Jenny Fretland VanVoorst.
Description: Minneapolis, MN: Jump!, Inc. [2017]
Series: Bullfrog books. What happens in winter?
"Bullfrog Books are published by Jump!."
Audience: Ages 5–8. | Audience: K to grade 3.
Includes bibliographical references and index.
Identifiers: LCCN 2016002933
ISBN 9781620313961 (hardcover: alk. paper)
ISBN 9781620315002 (paperback)
ISBN 9781624964435 (ebook)
Subjects:
LCSH: Weather—Juvenile literature.
Winter—Juvenile literature.
Classification:
LCC QB637.8.F74 2017 | DDC 508.2—dc23
LC record available at http://lccn.loc.gov/2016002933

Series Designer: Ellen Huber
Book Designer: Leah Sanders
Photo Researcher: Kirsten Chang

Photo Credits: All photos by Shutterstock except: Getty Images, 8–9, 24; Glow Images, 20–21; iStock, cover, 12–13, 23bl; Thinkstock, 10, 14–15, 16, 17, 22bl, 23tl, 23tr.

Printed in the United States of America at Corporate Graphics in North Mankato, Minnesota.

Table of Contents

Wintry Wonderland

Winter is here.

The trees have
lost their leaves.

5

The sky looks white.
Why?
The clouds are
full of snow.

The snow falls quickly.
Let's play outside!

The air is cold.

You need to wear a coat.

Ben puts on gloves.

He puts on a hat.

Ben and Dev go sledding.
Whee!

11

Sometimes the snow
is light and fluffy.

Will goes for a walk.

He catches a snowflake
on his tongue.

Sometimes the snow is wet. It is heavy.

It makes good snowballs.

Viv and Mia have a snowball fight.

Winter wind blows.

The snow flies. It drifts.

It covers the sidewalk.

Time to shovel!

Water freezes into ice.

Meg skates on
the icy pond.

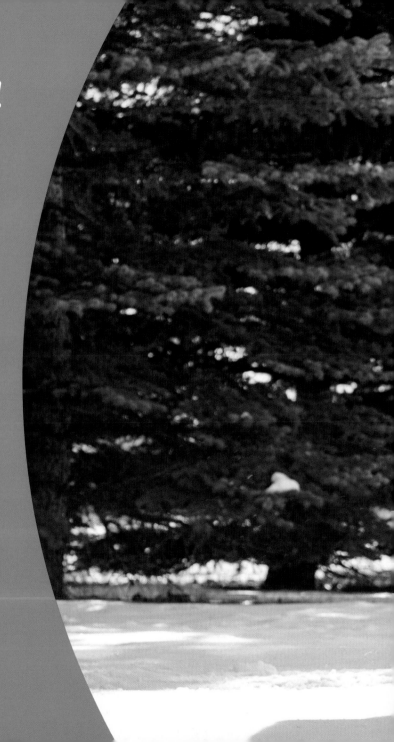

Winter is fun!

Water in Winter

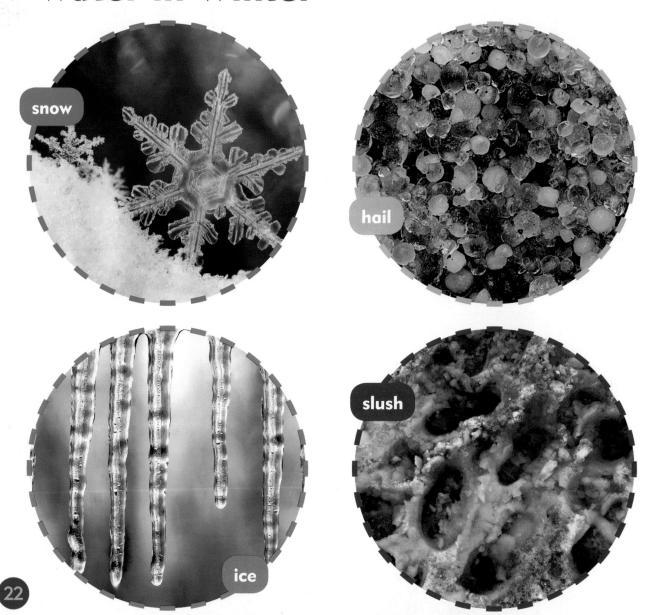

snow

hail

ice

slush

Picture Glossary

drift
To be driven along by a current of water, wind, or air.

snowball
A round mass of snow pressed or rolled together.

fluffy
Being light and soft or airy.

snowflake
A flake or crystal of snow.

Index

To Learn More

Learning more is as easy as 1, 2, 3.

1) Go to www.factsurfer.com

2) Enter "weatherinwinter" into the search box.

3) Click the "Surf" button to see a list of websites.

With factsurfer.com, finding more information is just a click away.